Explore-A-Province in China®

Shandong

OCDF Publications

OCDF Publications

is a division of Our Chinese Daughters Foundation (OCDF), a 501c3 non-profit organization, based in Bloomington, IL USA and Beijing, China. OCDF is dedicated to providing high quality culture programs and publications to children, teenagers, parents, and educators. Find us online at *www.ocdf.org/publications*.

Lead writers
Paris Lambrou
Diana Lambrou
Suí Hóng 隋宏

Editors
Dr. Jane Liedtke
Sharon Nakhimovsky
Megan Zaroda

Researchers
Bīngmǎ 冰马
Wáng Yúnhóng 王云洪

Design
Jonathan Tsao, Chinabeat Ltd.

Project Manager
Suí Hóng 隋宏

Project Developed By
Dr. Jane Liedtke

ISBN-13: 978-1-934487-52-5
ISBN-10: 1-934487-52-X

Copyright © 2009 by OCDF Publications, a division of Our Chinese Daughters Foundation, Inc.

Maps Copyright © 2007 held by the Chengdu Cartographic Publishing House

Educators are welcome to request from OCDF Publications complimentary teaching support materials that accompany this book. Please email: OCDFPublications@ocdf.org

Although the authors and OCDF Publications have taken all reasonable care in preparing this book, we make no guarantee about the accuracy or completeness of its content and, to the maximum extent permitted, disclaim all liability arising from its use.

All rights reserved. No part of this book may be reproduced or transmitted in any form or by any means, electronic or mechanical, including photocopying, recording, or by any information storage and retrieval system, without permission in writing from the Publisher.

Contents

Overview	8		Socioeconomy	16
Shandong Brief			*Economics Chat*	
Resources	10		Capital	20
Nature Notes			*Experiencing Jinan*	
History	12		People	24
Shandong Rewind			*An Oral Portrait*	

Heritage	28		Handy Tools	
Philosophy	28		*Map of Shandong*	5
Literature	30		*Map of Jinan*	6
Folk Arts	36		*References*	62
Technology and Medicine	38			
Tradition	64		Acknowledgements	63

Special Feature   48
The Story of Confucius

Highlights   50
Destinations   50
Local Flavors   58
Collector's Corner   60

A boy living in a western Shandong village is lighting some fireworks to celebrate the Chinese New Year, which is known as the Spring Festival.

Introduction

For the vast majority of Westerners, China has remained a mystery that is centuries old. China is enormous. Coupled with its 5,000-year history of traditions, the country has demonstrated that it is both quick to change, yet slow to relinquish its traditional values. Every year, China continues to attract visitors from all over the world. Some come to crack the riddle of Chinese culture; some are sent on business ventures; still others make the trip for the pure excitement of the place. And, there are those who fall in love with the country and decide to make a life there.

Modern China rests on the fulcrum between fantasy and reality. The growing interest in China, especially among the younger generation, has accelerated to form a "China Wave." Anything that is China-related is pursued with vigor: the language, the culture, the history, the food, and the people.

As the fascination with China's past, present, and future grows, visitors are exploring every facet of its mosaic of indigenous cultures, languages and customs. Each visitor leaves with his or her own impressions of the country, leaving the riddle intact. They return home with an open invitation to try China again and discover it anew as China changes.

One summer, Emma, a high school student from Chicago, Illinois in the USA, embarked on a journey to the Far East. She had studied Chinese for two years prior to her departure and had become passionate about anything and everything Chinese. As part of an exchange program, she was set to make a whirlwind summer tour of eastern China, particularly Ānhuī 安徽, Shànghǎi 上海, Shāndōng 山东, Zhèjiāng 浙江, Jiāngsū 江苏, Jiāngxī 江西, and Fújiàn 福建 provinces. Having already toured Ānhuī and Shànghǎi, her next stop was Shāndōng. In no time, she would be exploring the sacred mountains of Tàishān 泰山 (Mt. Tài), Qūfǔ 曲阜 (the birthplace of Confucius), and the province's rich folk arts. In due time, she would find herself expanding her cultural knowledge by reading *The Analects* by Confucius, walking the ancient city of Zībó 淄博 and learning about the carpentry tools invented by Lǔ Bān 鲁班.

Let's embark on this wonderful journey with Emma and see where her experiences lead her.

3

Explore-A-Province in China®

Legend 图例

政区图图例
Administrative Map Legend

★ 北京 Beijing	首都 Capital	特别行政区界	Special administrative zone boundary	1256	高程注记 Elevation in metres
◎ 南京 Nanjing	省级行政中心 Provincial-level administrative center		地区界 Regional boundary	大巴山 Dabashan Mt.	山脉名 Mountain
◎ 镇江 Zhenjiang	地级行政中心 Prefecture-level administrative center		军事分界线 Military demarcation line	台湾岛 Taiwan Is.	岛屿 Island
⊙ 六合 Liuhe	县级行政中心 County-level administrative center		高速公路 Highway	塔里木盆地 Tarim Basin	盆地 Basin
○ 谢集 Xieji	一般居民地 Local-level administrative center		国道 National highway	腾格里沙漠 Tenggeli Desert	沙漠 Desert
◎ 平壤 P'yŏngyang	外国首都 Foreign capital		一般公路 Road		
◎ 新义州 Sinŭiju	外国大中城市 Foreign large and medium size city		铁路 Railroad	—125—	经纬线 Longitude, latitude
○ 沙里院 Sariwŏn	外国一般城市 Foreign city		通航河段 Canal	北回归线 Tropic of cancer	北回归线 Tropic of Cancer
	国界、未定国界 National boundary Undefined international boundary	✈ 双流国际机场 Shuangliu International Airport	机场 Airport	至马尼拉1565海里 To Manila 1565n miles	航海线 Shipping route
	省级界 Provincial boundary	⚓ 天津港 Tianjin pt.	港口 Port	⛫ 长城 Great Wall	世界自然和文化遗产 UNESCO World Natural and Cultural Heritage Site
	河流、湖泊 River and lake	▲ 泰山 Taishan hill	山峰 Summit	🍁 九寨沟 Jiuzhaigou	国家重点风景名胜区 National scenic area

城市平面图
City Map Legend

★ 省政府 Provincial GOV.	省政府 Provincial government	白鹭洲公园 Bailuzhou Park	公园绿地 Park, green belt	商	商场 Mall, shopping center
★ 市政府 City Gov.	市政府 Municipal government	钟山风景区 Zhongshan Scenic Area	风景区 Scenic area	电	电信 Telecommunication center
★ 鼓楼区政府 Gulou section Gov.	市、区、县政府 Town (district, county) government	✚ 喇嘛庙 Lama Temple	风景点 Scenic spot	🚌	汽车站 Bus station
中山东路 East Zhongshan Rd.	一级街道 Primary road	潜洲 Qianzhou	地名 Place	🚉	火车站 Railway station
户部街 Hubu St.	二级街道 Secondary road	▲ 泰山 Taishan hill	山峰 Peak	🏨	宾馆 Hotel
太平门路 Taipingmen Rd.	三级街道 Tertiary road	东南大学 Southeast college	学校 School	🍴	餐厅 Restaurant
太平门路 Taipingmen Rd.	规划街道 Road under construction	🏦	银行 Bank	⚰	墓 Tomb
	铁路 Railroad	✛	医院 Hospital	🎬	电影院 Cinema

4

山东省地图
MAP OF SHANDONG PROVINCE

比例尺 Scale 1:2 700 000

济南地图

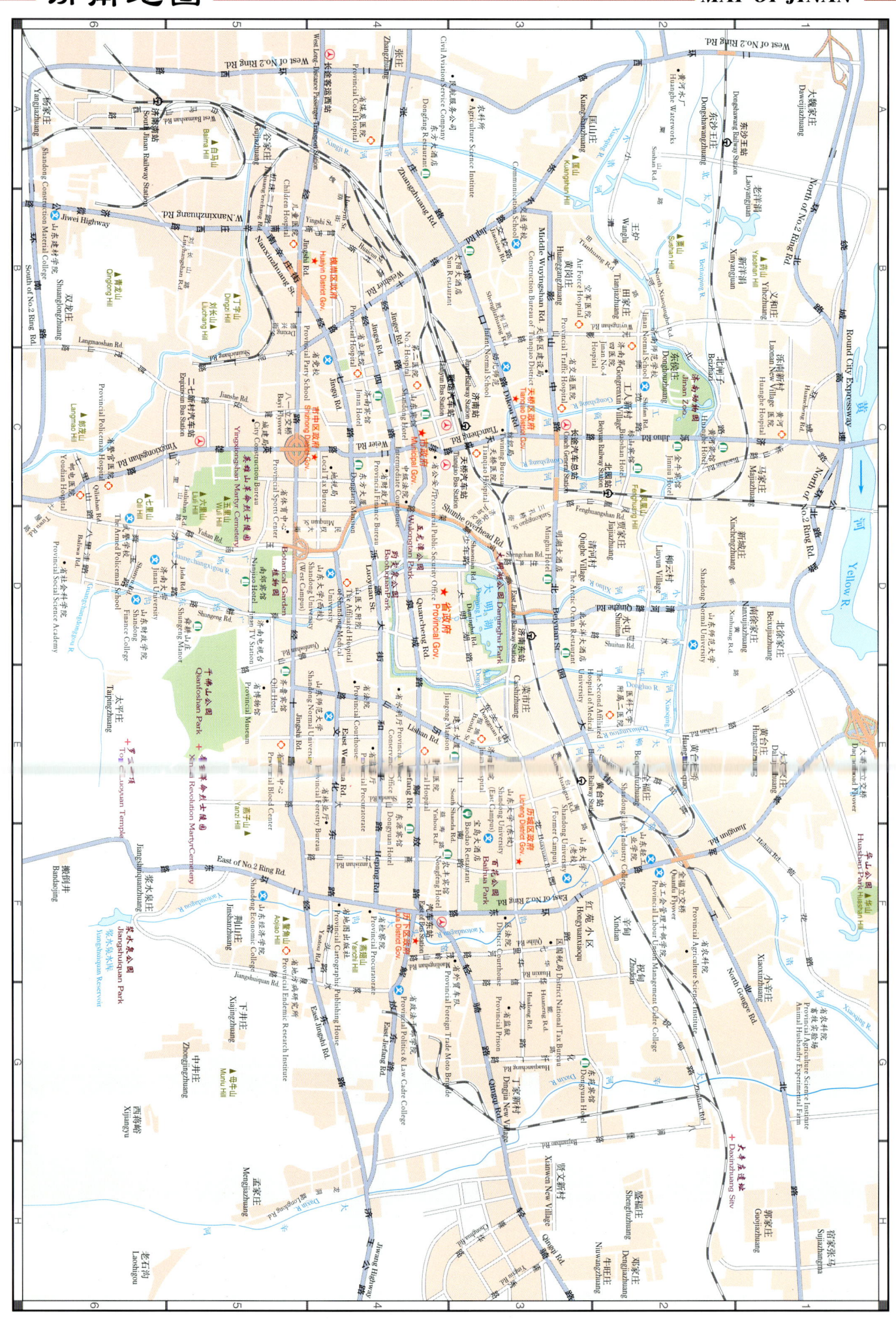

MAP OF JINAN

Jinan, the provincial capital of Shandong, is surrounded by a park.

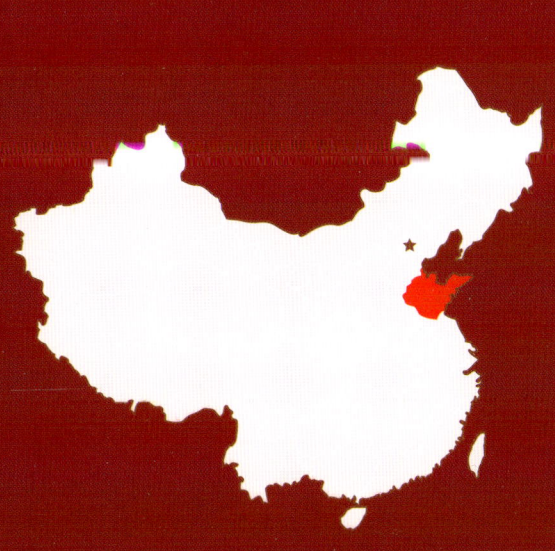

Shandong Province is located in China's eastern coastal region where the Yellow River flows into the Bohai Sea. The provincial capital is Jinan.

The Daimiao Temple at the foot of Taishan is where Chinese emperors offered sacrifices to Heaven and Earth.

Provincial Overview

Taishan, one of China's most popular mountains, has been a destination for many Chinese rulers since the Qin Dynasty. Today it's a UNESCO World Heritage Site.

Shandong in Brief

Origin

Shāndōng 山东 Province was officially established in the Qīng 清 Dynasty (1616 - 1911). During the Spring and Autumn Period (770 - 476 B.C.E.) and the Warring States Period (475 - 221 B.C.E.), the region was ruled by the State of Qí 齐 and the State of Lǔ 鲁. "Shāndōng" first came into being because the land was east of the Tàiháng Shān 太行山 (mountains). In ancient times, the two states, Qí and Lǔ greatly influenced Chinese history in terms of politics, culture, and economy. Therefore, Shāndōng Province has long been called "the Land of Qí and Lǔ" or just "Lǔ" for short.

Administrative Division

Shāndōng Province is located in China's eastern coastal region where the Yellow River flows into the Bóhǎi 渤海 Sea. The province also borders the Yellow Sea to the east, Héběi 河北 Province to the northwest, Hénán 河南 Province to the southwest, Ānhuī 安徽 Province and Jiāngsū 江苏 Province to the south. It covers an area of 160,000 sq km, comprising 1.6% of China's total territory. It spans 420 km from north to south and 700 km from east to west. The province is composed of 17 prefecture-level cities, 31 county-level cites, 60 counties and 49 municipal districts.

Population

The population of Shāndōng is over 92.12 million, the second largest after Hénán Province. The majority of the population is Hàn 汉, with minorities composing 1% of the total population. The major ethnic minority groups are the Huí 回, the Manchu, and the Zhuàng 壮.

The Capital

The provincial capital is Jǐnán 济南. The city is the political, economic, and cultural center of Shāndōng, as well as one of China's most famous historic and cultural cities. Jǐnán has an area of 8,177 sq km. The city has a population of 5.96 million people. Historically known for its many springs, Jǐnán has another name called quán chéng 泉城 which means the "City of Springs."

Terrain

Shāndōng borders ocean in the east and land in the west, and is criss-crossed with rivers and lakes. There are over 100 rivers longer than 50 km. The Yellow River, dubbed the "Mother River of the Chinese Nation," ends its long journey here and rushes to the Bóhǎi Sea. The famous Běijīng-Hángzhōu 北京 - 杭州 Grand Canal flows about 630 km from the southeast to the northwest through the plains of western Shāndōng. The four main lakes in the south, Wēishān 微山, Zhāoyáng 昭阳, Dúshān 独山, and Nányáng 南阳 lakes, are among the 10 largest freshwater lakes in China. The central part of Shāndōng is mountainous. Major mountains in the province include Tàishān 泰山 (also known as Mt. Tài), Méngshān 蒙山, Láoshān 崂山, Lǔshān 鲁山, and Yíshān 沂山.

Shaped like the beak of an eagle, the Shāndōng Peninsula boasts a coastline of 3,024 km, which is one sixth of the country's total. Shāndōng's location makes the province a juncture between north China and east China.

Climate

Shāndōng has a moderate climate, featured by distinctive seasons. In spring, the weather changes easily, ranging from drought to light rain or sandstorms. In summer, extremely hot and dry weather prevails. In autumn, the weather is dry and pleasant, while during the winter, it is cold and dry. The annual average temperature is

Considered the "Mother River of the Chinese Nation," the Yellow River stretches 5,500 km and runs through nine provinces and autonomous regions. It ends its journey in Shandong at the Bohai Sea.

In Shandong, kites, paper cuts, new year woodblock prints, and clay toys are common folk arts.

11 - 14°C, with an average precipitation level of 550 - 950 mm per year.

History and Culture

With remains of the Dàwènkǒu 大汶口 and Lóngshān 龙山 cultures, Shāndōng is considered one of the birthplaces of Chinese civilization. Until the Northern Sòng 宋 Dynasty (960 - 1127 C.E.), Shāndōng was the political and economic center of China. The Great Wall built by the State of Qí 齐 was several hundred years older than the one built during the Qín 秦 Dynasty (221 - 206 B.C.E.). According to the recent archeological discoveries, the earliest evidence of the written Chinese language was found in Shāndōng. The province is also the birthplace of china and silk.

Shāndōng is also known as the home province of Confucius and Mencius.

China's most renowned philosopher, Confucius (551 - 479 B.C.E.), is a native of Qufu, Shandong. Known as a hallowed place for Confucianism, Qufu is home to the Temple and Cemetery of Confucius and the Kong Family Mansion.

Confucius or Kǒng Zǐ 孔子, probably the most influential person in Chinese culture, is a native of Qūfǔ 曲阜, Shāndōng. Confucianism, considered the pillar of traditional Chinese society, was mainly developed by Confucius and his followers from Shāndōng. Apart from the great Confucian thinkers, numerous prominent historical figures also came from Shāndōng. They include Sūn Zǐ 孙子 (author of *The Art of War*), Mò Zǐ 墨子 (founder of Mohism), Lǔ Bān 鲁班 (great architect and founder of carpentry), Biǎn Què 扁鹊 (first traditional Chinese medicine doctor), and Zhūgě Liàng 诸葛亮 (wise man and great leader during the Three Kingdoms Period).

Shāndōng is rich in folk arts and crafts as well. Throughout the province, one can find traditional items like the kites of Wéifāng 潍坊, the pottery of Zībó 淄博, new year woodblock pictures of Yángjiābù 杨家埠, paper cuts and lovely toys.

Shāndōng's cooking style, known as Lǔcài 鲁菜, is considered one of the eight great traditions of Chinese cuisine. It has greatly influenced cooking in northern China.

Tourism

Visit Shandong for its beautiful natural scenery and historic sites, including Tàishān and the city of Qūfǔ, which are both UNESCO World Heritage Sites. Other places of interest are Wéifāng, the world-renowned capital for kites, Qīngdǎo 青岛, the Pearl of Yellow Sea, and Yāntái 烟台, famous for its pianos. Shāndōng is also known for its top quality wines.

Once a German colony, the port city of Qingdao has cobbled streets, red roof tiles, and seaside villas. It was the host city for the sailing competitions of the 2008 Olympics.

Fast Facts

Formal Name: Shāndōng 山东 Province

Abbreviation: Lǔ 鲁

Capital: Jǐnán 济南

Symbols:
Flower: Peony or mǔdān 牡丹

Land Size: Shāndōng has a landmass of 160,000 sq km, roughly the size of the country Tunisia.

Location: The lower reaches of the Yellow River, eastern China

Border Provinces: Héběi, Hénán, Ānhuī, Jiāngsū

Population: 92.12 million (2007)

Famous For: Tàishān, Confucius, Qūfǔ, Qīngdǎo, Wéifāng, local folk art, and the novel, *Outlaws of the Marsh*

Language: Mandarin (Pǔtōng huà 普通话) Chinese, Shāndōng huà 山东话 (local dialect)

Birthday Blessings

In China, to celebrate the birthday of a person who is over 60, one would say to him or her, "Wish you happiness as boundless as the East Sea and longevity as high as the South Mountain" (fú rú Dōnghǎi, shòu bǐ Nánshān 福如东海, 寿比南山.) In fact, according to some Chinese scholars, Dōnghǎi is the old name for the Bóhǎi 渤海 Sea, and Nánshān is today's Yúnmén Shān 云门山, located in Qīngzhōu 青州, Shāndōng 山东. On this mountain, there is a large character of shòu 寿 (longevity), 7.5 m x 3.7 m, which was carved during the Míng 明 Dynasty (1368 - 1644).

A large Chinese character, shou, meaning long life was inscribed on Yunmen Shan during the Ming Dynasty.

On his or her birthday, an elderly person is usually served longevity noodles, or shòumiàn 寿面, and buns made in the shape of peaches called shòutáo 寿桃 as a blessing. He or she is addressed as lǎo shòuxīng 老寿星, meaning someone who enjoys a long life.

Ancient Chinese coins with birthday blessings

Provincial Resources

Nature Notes

In some of Shandong's lake areas, fishermen train cormorants (dark-colored seabirds) to catch fish. Ropes are tied around cormorants' long necks to make sure they don't swallow the prey when they are fishing.

To be born and grow up in Shāndōng 山东 Province is wonderful. Without spending a lot of money, you can get a variety of fresh vegetables and fruit, as well as enjoy an abundant variety of seafood all year round.

Plants and Animals

A mild climate, a reasonable amount of rain, and rich soil enables Shāndōng to foster a considerable amount of plants and animals.

- You can find 3,100 different kinds of plants
- Over 90 different kinds of fruit trees are grown in the province
- Over 450 kinds of animal species have been identified
- Many kinds of butterflies live there
- Birds fly from the north to spend the winter there

Agriculture

Historically, agriculture has always been the pillar of development for Shāndōng. To this day, the province has been labeled "the barn of grains,

A mother and a daughter are embroidering shoe mats. They live in mountainous western Shandong where the climate and the soil are suitable for growing corn.

Along the eastern coastline, thousands of ladies, both young and old, are hired to collect kelp, a mass of large seaweed. Many of these ladies travel far from their home provinces to make money via short-term jobs.

cotton, and edible oil, and the big village of fruits and aquatic products." Shāndōng is the

- largest producer and exporter of peanuts
- largest producer of apples, pears, peaches, apricots, dates, grapes, and watermelon

MINERALS

Shāndōng is rich in some mineral resources that are of national importance. The province has extensive petroleum deposits, mainly in the Dōngyíng 东营 area.

- 128 different kinds of minerals
- The most plentiful natural resources are oil (ranks the second in the country), coal, iron ore, and sulfur
- The biggest producer of gold, diamonds, and sapphires in China

MARINE RESOURCES

With a long coastline, second after Guǎngdōng 广东, Shāndōng has rich marine resources with over 260 kinds of marine animals. The harvesting of abalone, prawns, scallops, and sea urchins all rank first in the country. Shāndōng is also the biggest producer of sea salt.

Because of its long coastline, Shandong abounds in marine resources like squid. In this photo, the fishermen are taking the squid out to dry.

Shandong is the biggest producer of sapphires in China.

Shouguang, the Hometown of Vegetables in China

The city of Shòuguāng 寿光 under Wéifāng's 潍坊 administration is historically known as a base of grains, vegetables, fruits, sea salt, and marine products. The earliest Chinese book on agriculture, *Important Arts for the People's Welfare* or Qí Mín Yào Shù 齐民要术, written during the Southern and Northern Dynasties (420 - 589 C.E.), talked at length about the experiences that people had in farming, fishing and weaving in the middle and lower reaches of the Yellow River, including today's Shòuguāng. The author of the book, Jiǎ Sīxié 贾思勰, was a Shòuguāng native and studied agriculture in the vicinity for many years.

Today, Shòuguāng is regarded as the Hometown of Vegetables in China and is labeled China's Silicon Valley of Ecological High-tech for Agriculture. It is here that the winter green-house was first designed. Soon after, it spread throughout northern China. Many Chinese people have benefited from this technology that allowed them enjoy fresh vegetables in all seasons. Before, people could only buy vegetables like cabbage and potatoes at local markets. Furthermore, millions of farmers got rich by setting up winter green houses and growing vegetables. Such large-scale farms can be seen in Shòuguāng. Equipped with the most advanced agricultural technology of the day, farmers produce pesticide-free produce welcomed all around the world. Visiting the Shòuguāng International Vegetable Expo, held between April and May each year, is really fun. You can see for yourself how the farmers in Shòuguāng, as well as those across China, have turned planting into a form of art.

Shouguang is famous for hosting the Shouguang International Vegetable Expo held during April and May each year.

Provincial History

Shandong Rewind

S: Sūn Zǐ 孙子 (who lived around the same time as Confucius), author of *The Art of War*, a native of Shāndōng 山东 Province
E: Emma, a high school student from Chicago, Illinois, USA

Standing on the very top of Tàishān 泰山 (Mt. Tài), two days after her arrival in Shāndōng, Emma was daydreaming, amidst the summer breeze and the fragrance of pine trees. In her dream, she found herself talking to a man dressed in a simple linen robe. He was writing something on bamboo slips, which was bamboo cut into pieces used as writing material before the Hàn 汉 Dynasty.

E: Wow, you look so cool! Which dynasty are you from? Who are you anyway?

S: Take a guess. I'm the one who says, "If you know your enemies and know yourself, you'll win a hundred times in a hundred battles."

E: Oh, my goodness, you're Sūn Zǐ, the author of the internationally renowned book, *The Art of War* or Sūn Zǐ Bīngfǎ 孙子兵法. I'm so lucky to meet you on this trip to Shāndōng. Maybe you could tell me something interesting about this place. All I knew before I came was that Shāndōng is the home to many great figures in Chinese history, and is famous for Tàishān where I'm standing. One of its coastal cities, Qīngdǎo 青岛, was a location for the 2008 Olympic Games. From my limited knowledge of the province, Shāndōng seems to be culturally rich.

S: Yes, that's absolutely true. Let me tell you more about Shāndōng's cultural roots. At the beginning, Shāndōng was inhabited by the people of Dōng Yí 东夷, a people skilled in using bows and arrows. One interesting thing to note about them is that they were taller than most other Chinese people.

You must have read a Chinese myth about a man named Hòu Yì 后羿, who shot down nine suns, and another man by the name of Fú Xī 伏羲, who invented the Eight Trigrams or bāguà 八卦. These men are both Shāndōng natives. There is another important figure you should know about: Chī Yóu 蚩尤, who was a powerful leader of many tribes of Dōng Yí. He lived around 2700 B.C.E., the time when the Yellow Emperor or Huáng Dì 黄帝 reigned. He was very skilled at making metal weapons, and so he is regarded by many as the Father of Chinese Weapons.

E: Chī Yóu, I know him. He had a big fight with the Yellow Emperor and the Emperor Yán Dì 炎帝 at a place called Zhuōlù 涿鹿 in today's Héběi 河北 Province. He was defeated and killed.

S: Oh, you've already learned quite a lot! I'm impressed. After the battle, some people from the Dōng Yí tribes moved southward and settled down in various places in today's Húnán 湖南, Guìzhōu 贵州, and Yúnnán 云南 provinces. These people later became known as the Miáo 苗 minority of China.

E: That's interesting to know. Were there any Chinese emperors from Shāndōng? I always like to hear stories about them.

S: Interestingly, there wasn't a single emperor from Shāndōng. This fact tells something about the nature of the Shāndōng people. So influenced by the teachings of one of my contemporaries, Confucius or Kǒng Zǐ 孔子, people didn't dare question authorities or the mandate. The tendency to obey was embedded in our nature. Even during bad times when people couldn't face harsh realities like tyranny, for instance, they rebelled, only hoping to replace the bad officials with the good ones. However, they never thought that they could be emperors themselves. Having such an idea was totally against the culture in which they were raised. To say "no" to an emperor is like saying "no" to one's father, and that was considered a serious crime. That explains why there were so many farmers' uprisings, but there wasn't one case that any of their leaders became emperors.

E: I suppose it's difficult to understand this from a Western perspective. But if there were no emperors from Shāndōng, why did so many emperors pay attention to Tàishān?

S: Coming to Tàishān to pay tribute to heaven is an old tradition dating back to the sage king Shùn 舜. Holding a ceremony here allowed emperors to show the world that they ruled with the mandate from heaven, and they were heaven's sons or tiānzǐ 天子. Confucius reinforced this idea when he talked about relationships. He emphasized obedience in relationships like subject to emperor, son to father, wife to husband, younger brother to elder brother, and younger friend to elder friend.

E: I know that Confucianism has been the orthodox teaching in China since the Hàn 汉 Dynasty (206 B.C.E. - 220 C.E.). From what you've just said, I wonder why Shāndōng was especially affected by Confucian dogma?

S: Shāndōng has always been an agricultural province. Due to the fact

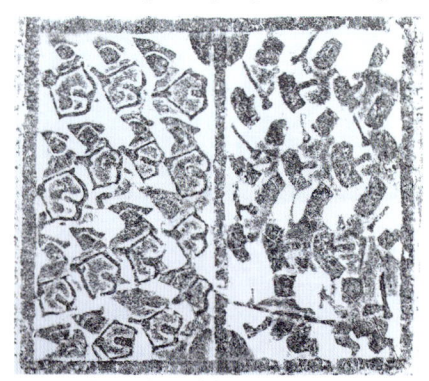

Dong Yi people with bows and arrows on a Han Dynasty bas-relief. They were the earliest inhabitants of Shandong and were the first to invent the bow in China.

Sun Zi, author of "The Art of War"

that the majority of its people have been farmers, the province is still deeply affected by Confucianism, which has a history of looking down on commercialism and people involved in commerce. This has shaped the history and society of Shāndōng much more than you might think. As a result, Shāndōng's business sector didn't compare to those of Shānxī 山西, Ānhuī 安徽, Zhèjiāng 浙江, Jiāngsū 江苏 and Guǎngdōng 广东. People in Shāndōng didn't like to make long journeys to trade goods. They held the Confucian belief that if one's parents are alive, one shouldn't travel far. Thus, even during the times of the Míng 明 and Qīng 清 dynasties, when business flourished along the Grand Canal, the many shops were actually owned by businessmen from Shānxī and Ānhuī provinces.

E: I see now that Confucianism is quite double-edged. But I hear that many families left the province and migrated to the northeast.

S: Yes, this kind of migration started in the Qīng Dynasty (1616 - 1911). The Qīng Dynasty was founded by a northeastern people called the Manchurians. By the 17th century, the Manchurians occupied much of China, but the vast area where they came from was sparsely populated. So the Qīng Court decided to move people from densely populated areas to the northeast. Most of the people who migrated were from Shāndōng, and this move is called chuǎng guāndōng 闯关东. If you travel to Dàlián 大连, a coastal city in Liáoníng 辽宁 Province, you will probably notice the dialect is very similar to that of eastern Shāndōng.

Photo taken prior to migration. Beginning in the Qing Dynasty (1616 - 1911), many people from Shandong migrated to the northeastern part of China, namely Heilongjiang, Jilin, and Liaoning provinces.

Jiang Taigong Who Fished and Waited

During the 11th century B.C.E., there lived in Shāndōng 山东 a wise man called Jiāng Tàigōng 姜太公 (also known as Jiāng Zǐyá 姜子牙 or Jiāng Shàng 姜尚). By that time, much of today's China was ruled by the tyrants of the Shāng 商 Dynasty (1600 - 1046 B.C.E.). Though a military strategist and eager to overthrow the Shāng kings, Jiāng Tàigōng was patient enough to wait until he found the right person to assist. During this waiting period, he spent most of his days fishing at the Wèihé 渭河 River (near today's Xī'ān 西安, Shaanxi Province). When he reached the age of 80, he was still fishing and still waiting. One day King Wén 文 of the Western Zhōu 周 Dynasty (1046 - 256 B.C.E.) came across Jiāng Tàigōng fishing without bait. The king immediately recognized his talents and took him back to be his prime minister. A familiar saying is derived from this story: Jiāng Tàigōng cast a hookless and baitless line for the fish that wanted to be caught (Jiāng Tàigōng diàoyú, yuànzhě shànggōu 姜太公钓鱼，愿者上钩). It means that if one waits long enough, things will come his or her way.

After the Zhōu people overthrew the Shāng Dynasty, Jiāng Tàigōng was made the first duke of the State of Qí 齐 (today's eastern Shāndōng). There Jiāng Tàigōng fully exercised his belief that a state could become powerful only when its people prospered. A capable governor, he cut taxes, favored commercialism, and promoted the development of agriculture, weaving, and metal work. The State of Qí soon became the strongest and richest of all states. Jiāng Tàigōng has been remembered through the ages for his talent both as a military strategist and an administrator. A popular Chinese novel called *Tales of Gods and Heroes* or Fēngshén Yǎnyì 封神演义 compiled in the Míng 明 Dynasty (1368 - 1644) was attributed to him.

Jiang Taigong is widely worshipped as a symbolic figure of wisdom in Chinese culture.

Xu Fu and Japan

After the first Chinese Emperor Qín Shǐ Huáng 秦始皇 unified China and founded the Qín 秦 Dynasty (221 - 206 B.C.E.), he became obsessed with the idea of death. He wanted to be immortal. He ordered many Daoist priests and sorcerers to search for immortals. These people allegedly lived on the east coast of China and held the secret for elixirs. When priests and sorcerers returned empty-handed, the emperor was furious and became even more desperate. At this time, Xú Fú 徐福, a sorcerer from Shāndōng, told Qín Shǐ Huáng that he could fulfill the mission if he was granted an army of men and women. The emperor agreed to give him 3,000 young people (500 of them were virgins,) together with a large crew of skilled tradespeople. Fully equipped with manpower and seeds of many kinds, Xú Fú bid the Emperor goodbye from Pénglái 蓬莱. He never returned. There is sufficient evidence, however, that he landed in Japan, at a place called Shingu in southern Wakayama. With what he got from Qín Shǐ Huáng, Xú Fú set himself up to work with the Japanese people and taught them to be better farmers and craftsmen.

The Boxer Rebellion first started in 1900 in Shandong. The Boxers rebelled against all foreign influence. Though quickly crushed by foreign troops, the Boxer Rebellion hastened the downfall of the Qing Dynasty.

E: What happened to Shāndōng after the fall of the Qīng Empire in 1911?

S: When Shāndōng was opened to foreign powers in the 19th century, the eastern part was mainly handed over to the Germans. Thus, there was a heavy German presence in Qīngdǎo and other coastal cities. With the collapse of the Qīng Empire, Japan assumed control of eastern Shāndōng. This led to a national protest which marked the beginning of the May Fourth Movement.

Shāndōng also suffered during the Japanese invasion between 1937 and 1945. You can read about this period of history in a highly-acclaimed novel called *The Red Sorghum* written by Mò Yán 莫言. The Japanese practiced a cruel policy here known as the Three Alls: burn all, kill all, and loot all. They were met with strong resistance from both the Communist Party and the Nationalist Party. The highest official who died heroically was a Shāndōng-born general named Zhāng Zìzhōng 张自忠 (1891 - 1940), a member of the Nationalist Party. After his death, roads in Běijīng 北京, Tiānjīn 天津 and Wǔhàn 武汉 were renamed in his honor.

E: One last question, were there any prominent women from Shāndōng?

S: Do you know who Madame Máo 毛 was?

E: I guess she was related to Chairman Máo Zédōng 毛泽东. Was she his wife?

S: Yes, she is the famed Jiāng Qīng 江青. Jiāng Qīng is the name she gave herself when she moved to Yán'ān 延安, the Communist base after 1935. Actually, she changed her name several times. She was born as Lǐ Yúnhè 李云鹤, but she called herself Lán Píng 蓝苹 when she became a second-rate starlet in Shànghǎi 上海. Though many Shāndōng locals were ashamed to admit that she was from Shāndōng, she is someone that history cannot ignore. This woman saw herself as another Wǔ Zétiān 武则天 (624 - 705 C.E.), the first and the only woman emperor in Chinese history, who had an unquenchable thirst for power. Jiāng Qīng's prime years were during the Cultural Revolution (1966 - 1976). Within this 10-year period, she took a strong hold on the cultural affairs and ideology of the country. She ordered that only plays and films with revolutionary themes be released to the public. After Máo's death, she and other high-ranking leaders were arrested; the infamous group was known as the Gang of Four. Sentenced to life imprisonment, she subsequently killed herself in 1991 at the age of 77.

E: Would it be cruel to say the Confucian maxim: "Inferior men and women are hard to raise?"

S: I'd rather you know another maxim supposedly said by the same man: "If something is disliked by all, it's indeed worth an investigation. If something is liked by all, it's indeed worth an investigation."

With that, Limma was wide awake, her face flushed in the summer heat. What a dream, she thought to herself.

A young couple from Junan County, Shandong, got married in 1966, the first year of the 10-year Cultural Revolution. The wedding gifts they received from the people's commune were a spade, a pickaxe and a Red Book of Chairman Mao's works.

Famous Political

Fáng Xuánlíng 房玄龄 (579 - 648 C. E.)

AKA: Fáng Qiáo 房乔
From: Línzī 临淄 City (today under Zībó's 淄博 administration), Shāndōng 山东
Known For: One of the most important prime ministers of the Táng 唐 Dynasty and an accomplished poet

Born into a well-established military family, Fáng Xuánlíng spent his youth educating himself and passed the imperial examination at age 17. He and his father became consultants to Lǐ Yuān 李渊 aiding his attempts to overthrow the Suí 隋 Emperor Yáng Dì 炀帝. After Lǐ Yuān took over China and founded the Táng Dynasty (618 - 907 C.E.), Fáng Xuánlíng continued his service to Prince Lǐ Shìmín 李世民. The two became close friends. Later Lǐ Shìmín took the throne and started his reign under the name Táng Tàizōng 唐太宗. He appointed Fáng Xuánlíng as his prime minister, who, in this post, worked 20 long years and was held in high regard by both the emperor and fellow colleagues. He was later regarded as a model for prime ministers and also seen as one of the 10 greatest prime ministers in history. After his death, his family suffered significant hardship: one of his three sons was executed, and the eldest son was demoted to country sheriff in modern day Guǎngdōng 广东. The famous Hong Kong kung fu star Jackie Chan or Chéng Lóng 成龙, whose real family name is also Fáng 房, believes he is a descendant of the prime minister.

Jackie Chan

Figures from Shandong

Jiāng Qīng 江青 (1914 - 1991)

AKA: Madame Máo 毛, Lǐ Yúnhè 李云鹤, Lán Píng 蓝苹
Birth: Zhūchéng 诸城 City, Shāndōng 山东
Known For: Wife of Chairman Máo Zédōng 毛泽东

Jiāng Qīng was born into a poor family. Her father was a carpenter, and her mother a housemaid. In 1931, at the age of 17, she was married to Péi Mínglún 裴明伦, a man from a rich family. The marriage ended in the same year. Between 1931 and 1933, she worked as a librarian at Qīngdǎo 青岛 University and lived with a Communist named Huáng Jìng 黄敬. She then began acting in some revolutionary plays. After Huáng Jìng was arrested by the Nationalist Party, Jiāng Qīng moved to Shànghǎi 上海 and starred in some revolutionary movies. Rumor has it that Jiāng Qīng, who was then known as Lán Píng, often quarreled with other actresses over roles and over men. After the Japanese invaded the eastern part of China in 1937, she settled in Yán'ān 延安, Shaanxi Province, a base for the Communist Party at that time. There, she worked as a drama instructor and was noticed by Máo Zédōng, who arranged to have her work as his personal secretary. The two were married one year later.

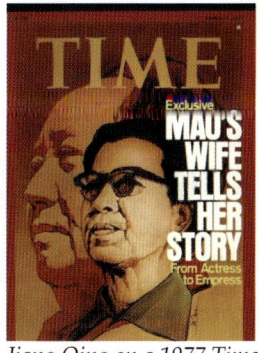

Jiang Qing on a 1977 Time Magazine cover

After the new republic was founded by the Communist Party in 1949, Jiāng Qīng almost disappeared in the eyes of the public. The Cultural Revolution, started by Chairman Máo himself, gave Jiāng Qīng the opportunity to function as well as to perish. She became a member of the Politburo in 1969 and was appointed Deputy Director of the Cultural Revolution. She was active in helping her husband purge his rivals such as Liú Shàoqí 刘少奇 and Dèng Xiǎopíng 邓小平. As the highest leader in charge of cultural activities, she ordered the purge of anything not Red (not Communist). She instructed that all works of art had to reflect the correctness and the greatness of Chairman Máo, her husband. During the 10 years of purification, there was hardly anything interesting in the cultural scene, except for the "Eight Revolutionary Model Plays. "

Jiāng Qīng's personal fall followed Máo's death in 1976. She was arrested and given a death sentence that was subsequently changed to life in prison. At one of her trials in 1981, she famously said, "I was Máo's mad dog. Whomever he asked me to bite, I bit." In saying these words, Jiāng Qīng tried to portray herself a scapegoat. Ten years later, in 1991, the woman who saw herself as the standard-bearer of the Cultural Revolution committed suicide.

Shandong Timeline

Paleolithic Period (2.5 million - 10000 B.C.E.)
- The Yíyuán 沂源 Ape Man lives

Neolithic Period (8000 - 2000 B.C.E.)
- The Dàwènkǒu 大汶口 Culture (4000 - 2600 B.C.E.)
- The Lóngshān 龙山 Culture (2900 - 2100 B.C.E.)
- Most of Shāndōng is populated by the Dōng Yí 东夷 tribes

Xià 夏 Dynasty (2070 - 1600 B.C.E.)

Shāng 商 Dynasty (1600 - 1046 B.C.E.)

Western Zhōu 周 Dynasty (1046 - 256 B.C.E)
- The states of Qí 齐 and Lǔ 鲁 are established in 1043 B.C.E.

Spring and Autumn Period (770 - 476 B.C.E.)
- The Qí Great Wall is built
- Confucius or Kǒng Zǐ 孔子 lives and teaches in Shāndōng

Warring States Period (475 - 221 B.C.E.)
- Mencius lives and teaches in Shāndōng

Qín 秦 Dynasty (221 - 206 B.C.E.)
- Qín unifies China
- Emperor Qín Shǐ Huáng 秦始皇 climbs Tàishān 泰山 (Mt. Tai)
- Xú Fú 徐福 sails to the sea and supposedly lands in Japan

Hàn 汉 Dynasty (206 B.C.E. - 220 C.E.)

Three Kingdoms (220 - 280 C.E.)
- Shāndōng is part of the Wèi 魏 Kingdom led by Cáo Cāo 曹操 and his son Cáo Pī 曹丕

Western Jìn 晋 (265 - 317 C.E.)
- Clans begin to move to southern China

Eastern Jìn (317 - 420 C.E.)

Southern and Northern Dynasties (420 - 589 C.E.)
- Over 400 Buddhist sculptures are made in Qīngzhōu 青州, Wéifāng 潍坊

Suí 隋 Dynasty (581 - 618 C.E.)
- The Grand Canal extending from Hángzhōu to Běijīng is built

Táng 唐 Dynasty (618 - 907 C.E.)
- A period of peace and stability - arts and literature flourish

Five Dynasties (907 - 960 C.E.)

Liáo 辽 Dynasty (916 - 1125 C.E.)

Sòng 宋 Dynasty (960 - 1279 C.E.)
- Foreigners invade northern China
- Large numbers of Hàn 汉 Chinese move to southern China
- The female poet Li Qīngzhào 李清照 lives
- Liángshānpō 梁山泊 uprising

Yuán 元 Dynasty (1206 - 1368)
- Shāndōng becomes part of the Mongol Empire

Míng 明 Dynasty (1368 - 1644)
- Many families migrate from Shānxī 山西 and settle in Shāndōng in the early Míng Dynasty
- Water transportation on the Grand Canal resumes, and as a result, many cities along the canal flourish
- The famous novel, *The Plum in the Golden Vase*, is popular

Qīng 清 Dynasty (1616 - 1911)
- Modern-day Shāndōng Province is formed
- Pú Sōnglíng 蒲松龄 finishes his collection of short stories, *Strange Tales from Make-Do Studio*
- Shāndōng people begin to immigrate to northeast China
- The Yellow Sea Battle also known as Jiǎ Wǔ 甲午 Sino-Japanese War is fought in 1894 -1895
- The Boxer Rebellion first breaks out in Shāndōng in 1899 and soon spreads to northern China
- Qīngdǎo 青岛 is occupied by Japan

The Republic of China (1912-1949)
- Much of Shāndōng is occupied by Japan between 1937 and 1945
- The Nationalist Party and the CPC fight in Shāndōng

The People's Republic of China (PRC) (1949 - Present)
- The Great Leap Forward (1958 - 1960)
- The Cultural Revolution (1966 - 1976)
- Chairman Máo's 毛 wife, Madame Máo or Jiāng Qīng 江青 is active during this period and later sentenced to life-long imprisonment. She commits suicide and dies in 1991.

Provincial Socioeconomy

Economics Chat

Workers on an oil field. Shandong has extensive petroleum deposits, mainly in the Dongying area.

E: Emma, a high school student from Chicago touring Shāndōng 山东
M: Xiǎo Mèng 小孟, a tour guide and Shāndōng native

Sitting in her Qīngdǎo 青岛 hotel room that overlooks the sea, Emma was both relaxed and contemplative. She had seen a lot of the province, and was deeply impressed by its development, its culture, and its food. She was wondering whether her "Shāndōng" was real, when her tour guide Xiǎo Mèng came to chat with her.

E: It's good that you came. I was just thinking about my trip. Everything that I see in Shāndōng seems so wonderful. Is that true or am I just dreaming?

M: It's very natural for a first-time visitor to Shāndōng to take a liking to the province. There is a popular joke in China that Shāndōng beats all the other provinces by only three things: one mountain (the Tàishān 泰山), one river (the Yellow River) and the one saint (Confucius). What Shāndōng has is very Chinese and very basic to Chinese culture, and thus very appealing to outside visitors.

E: I guess that tourism's big in Shāndōng?

M: That's very true. People come here for those three things I mentioned and more. The coastal areas and folk arts are big draws too.

E: You told me that Shāndōng ranks second or third in China's GDP (gross domestic product), after Guǎngdōng 广东 and Jiāngsū 江苏. Does tourism play a big role in Shāndōng's GDP?

M: Half true. The greatest contributors to the province's GDP are agricultural output, mineral production, transportation and large state-run enterprises. Shāndōng ranks first in its output of cotton and wheat as well as gold, diamonds, and sapphires. The province also has extensive petroleum deposits, mainly in the Dōngyíng 东营 area. The Shènglì 胜利 (Victory) Oilfield is one of the major oilfields in China. Thanks to its energy industry, Shāndōng is the only coastal province that doesn't have a cap on its electricity consumption. While enterprises in other provinces such as Guǎngdōng, Jiāngsū and Zhèjiāng 浙江 suffer from electricity shortages, Shāndōng is blessed with sufficient electricity, a premise for its speedy economic growth.

E: I also noticed that the roads here are very well-constructed, unlike the ones in Ānhuī 安徽 Province.

M: Speaking about the infrastructure, let me tell you something that visitors do not know about the highways. If you travel on a long-distance bus in China, you probably won't be able to sleep on the bus because of the disrepair and unevenness of the roads. Shāndōng, however, has the longest mileage of highways, all of which are continually repaired and well-maintained. The provincial government of Shāndōng also has a very strong hold in key economic areas such as infrastructure development and large-scale state-run corporations, such as Haier (manufacturer of home appliances), Hisense (manufacturer of televisions), Lǔ 鲁 Energy (Shāndōng Power Group), Kingsburg Piano (Yāntái 烟台), Tsingtao Beer and Zhāngyù 张裕 Wine. While state-run enterprises in the northeastern part of China suffer serious declines due to their inability to adapt to the market economy, Shāndōng's conglomerates are much healthier and enjoy more brand recognition.

E: I see that here in Qīngdǎo, there are many Korean shops and restaurants, so I guess there must be a large Korean community.

M: Yes, Koreans are in almost every major coastal city of Shāndōng, namely Qīngdǎo, Yāntái and Wēihǎi 威海. Actually Japan is also a key player in terms of foreign investment. This is because both countries are in close geographical proximity to Shāndōng, and because of this, labor is cheaper and the transportation costs are low.

E: One thing I love about Shāndōng is that there is such a variety of fresh fruits and vegetables. The apples and the pears are so juicy, sweet, and fragrant!

M: Enjoy this abundance while you're here. Shāndōng people are lucky to

A farmer in Zouping County makes extra money by selling miniature wheelbarrows.

Shandong is the largest producer of apples in China.

Farmers in a Shandong village are winnowing grain in front of a large portrait Chairman Mao. His image is more commonly seen in rural China than in urban areas today.

A farmer in western Shandong

A wine cellar in Yantai. Shandong produces the country's best wine. Yantai is the birthplace of China's first wine company (1892). As of 2007, over 10,000 hectares of land is used for vineyards.

Now a global brand, Haier, originally from Qingdao, is the world's fourth largest appliance manufacturer. The company has over 50,000 employees worldwide.

have such rich soil, such mild climate and such a long agricultural history. Shāndōng is a true powerhouse, serving as a backyard garden or as some say "the vegetable basket" for major cities like Běijīng 北京 and Shànghǎi 上海. If you travel from Jǐnán 济南 to coastal areas in winter, you'll see long stretches of indoor greenhouses that grow the best of the country's pesticide-free produce. Along the national highway between Yāntái and Pénglái 蓬莱, there are numerous vineyards that produce the best wine in China. The region is located at the same latitude as Bordeaux, France, and thus shares a similar climate equally good for growing grapes.

E: From what you've said, the farmers here must be very rich.

M: Economic development in Shāndōng is not very even. The east is much more developed and has more resources than the west does. The people in the west are deeply influenced by Confucian thinking and its take on commercialism. They have a long history of detesting business. So, in an era of changes, the people in the west need to be more open to reforms and equip themselves with business skills.

E: I feel the future of Shāndōng is very promising.

M: There is a saying in China that in the 1980s, everyone looked to Guǎngdōng, in the 1990s they looked to Pǔdōng 浦东 (Shànghǎi), and in the 21st century they'll watch Shāndōng. I'm confident we don't have to wait too long to make this happen.

Liang Xisen and His Home Village

Rows of plain looking villas in one of Shāndōng's 山东 poorest areas! A showcase of China's "new socialist countryside," Liángzhuī 梁锥 Village, Lèlíng 乐陵 City, has built over 100 villas, 280 sq m each, to give to its villagers. This was accomplished with the help of a large donation from property tycoon Liáng Xīsēn 梁希森. A Liángzhuī Village native, Liáng Xīsēn was born to a poor family and could barely read and write. But his humble background didn't prevent him from becoming a successful businessman.

His start came in 1986 from a small flour-processing factory in his home village. Over time, Liáng Xīsēn accumulated his immense wealth from a Běijīng 北京 villa development project called Rose Garden. After several waves of property developers, Liáng Xīsēn obtained the project cheaply in 1999. He invested some 70 million Yuán 元 to build 40 villas. These high-end villas soon became hot-ticket items, especially after it was announced that Běijīng would host the 2008 Olympic Games. Each villa was sold at a price of 160 million Yuán.

With the money he earned, Liáng Xīsēn redeveloped his home village. He built 136 villas for people over the age of 40, and apartment buildings for those under 40. In exchange, the farmers relinquished their farmland to Liáng Xīsēn and became workers on his 23-hectare beef feedlot and slaughterhouse, making a monthly salary of 700 Yuán each. The workers are also given shares in the farm and entitled to bonuses. With work and housing assured, most of the villagers prefer to stay in the village. Only a few farmers have left to live life as a migrant worker in a big city.

China's Political System and Government

China, through the ages has always been unique, in size, cultural diversity, world view and even its government. The vision of Máo Zédōng's 毛泽东 post-1949 "New China" spun the country into directions and alliances that were probably inconceivable to him as he set out on his vision to remake the nation as a "people's" government.

China's sheer size (9.6 million sq km) and home to over one fifth (1.3 billion people) of humanity demand a governance structure radically different from Western models. The structure of the government is not neatly divided into executive and administrative branches. Instead, there are several divisions and organizations which interact and oversee one another, but which are fundamentally driven from the top down. The "top down," with the near absence of a lateral interaction, is more than a characteristic of government, it is a reflection of the Chinese culture, its traditions, and development through the ages.

Head of State

The president, as head of state, signs laws into order, appoints the premier, vice premiers, state councilors, ministers of various ministries and state commissions, the auditor-general, and the secretary-general of the State Council. These appointments accord with the decisions of the National Peoples Congress (NPC) and its Standing Committee. As well as conferring honorary titles of State and issuing orders of special amnesty, the president has the power to declare martial law, declare a state of war, and announce orders of general mobilization of the people's military.

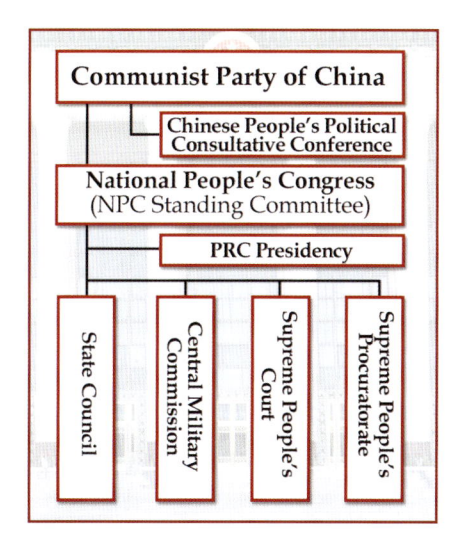

National People's Congress

The NPC is the governing organ of supreme power in the People's Republic of China. Its permanent body or group of leaders in office is called the Standing Committee. Both the NPC and its Standing Committee are elected for a term of five years through a process called "democratic centralism." A Chinese citizen exercises his or her right to vote at the local or county level, where elections determine the representatives or deputies to the NPC. Beyond the county level however, leadership positions are appointed (appointments are handed down by the next level of government, i.e. province to city, city to prefecture, prefecture to county). These appointments are ultimately subject to the NPC's approval. The NPC and its Standing Committee exercise the power of legislation, and in matters of election they retain the power to decide, supervise, appoint, and dismiss.

The State Council

The State Council, also known as the Central People's Government, is China's highest administrative body. It carries out the laws and decisions made by the NPC and is responsible for running the nation's day-to-day business. The State Council is made up of the premier, vice-premiers, state councilors and ministers. Once again, these appointments are subject to the NPC's approval.

The Communist Party of China (CPC) was founded in 1921 in Shànghǎi 上海. It has been the party in power since 1949 where, under the leadership of Chairman Máo Zédōng, the People's Republic of China declared its nationhood in Tiān'ānmén 天安门 Square on October 1st of the same year.

Although the CPC has both central and local organizations, the Central Committee stands at the top of the organizational structure. Its General Secretary and the President of China have been the same person since 1983. The CPC nominates its Party's General Secretary for the position of Head of State (President), the nomination goes to the NPC for approval. In addition to his role as General Secretary, the President acts as Chairman of the Armed Forces and is assisted by vice chairmen and a membership body under the title of **The Central Military Commission** of the PRC. The commission is elected for a term of five years after which its members can stand for re-election.

The Politburo (now 26 members) together with its Standing Committee undertakes the major decision-making of the CPC, as well as exercising the power of the Central Committee when that body is not in session. The CPC does not directly issue orders to organs of state power. What it does is put forward recommendations that are then exercised by the NPC.

A major advisory body to the CPC is **The Chinese People's Political Consultative Conference (CPPCC)**. It is a united front organization under the leadership of the Communist Party of China and includes the other eight non-communist parties. It also includes the **mass organizations** that represent groups within society such as the All-China Federation of Trade Unions, the Communist Youth League of China, and the All-China Women's Federation. These mass organizations basically function as liaisons between government, CPC, and the interest groups they represent, and work on a daily basis to benefit their constituencies. They meet annually in March or under special invitation from the CPC to draft white papers and submit suggestions to the Party and the State Council.

Local governments are responsible for running regional affairs and reporting to their superiors, i.e. county to prefecture to city to province to central government. Local democratic-style elections are held at the township and county levels enabling ordinary citizens to participate in governance.

Hong Kong and Macau are two special administrative regions which under "one country, two systems" function with more autonomy although in close contact with authorities in Běijīng 北京.

For the newcomer to all things Chinese, the barrage of government acronyms may seem confusing. The awkwardness can be accounted for however, when one visits this enormously diverse country where most people's lives are far from the government and politics of the capital. The day-to-day life of the average Chinese citizen is very much a product of Confucian ideals and operates from a distinctly Eastern sense of logic.

Provincial Capital

Experiencing Jinan

The Spring City Square, located in the heart of the city, showcases the modern development of Jinan. The city invested 1.3 billion Yuan to complete the square.

The capital of Shāndōng 山东 Province, Jǐnán 济南 is the political, economic, and cultural center of the province. For several decades the city has been known to have the lowest crime rate in China.

Geography and Climate

Jǐnán lies in midwest Shāndōng, just three miles south of the Yellow River and very near the foot of Mt. Tài or Tàishān 泰山. The terrain slopes down from south to north. The city has a semi-humid continental monsoon climate, and is hot in the summer and cold in the winter. Spring and autumn are short, but the weather is usually nice. The average temperature is 13.6 °C, and the mean precipitation level is 614 mm.

The old and picturesque side of Jinan is still well-preserved.

History

In ancient times, Jinan was situated to the south of Jǐ 济 River, which is now a part of the Yellow River. That is how Jǐnán got its name, which means south of Jǐ River. Historical and cultural remnants show that various tribes lived in the area from 4,000 B.C.E. onwards. They made fine black pottery and invented a unique way of writing prior to the famous oracle bone inscriptions. Their culture was known as the Lóngshān 龙山 Culture. During the Táng 唐 (618 - 907 C.E.) and Sòng 宋 (960 - 1279 C.E.) dynasties, Jǐnán developed into an important city due to its location near the Grand Canal or dà yùnhé 大运河. Construction of this canal began in the Suí 隋 Dynasty (581 - 618 C.E.), and was completed in the 13th century. Eventually, the canal that connected Běijīng 北京 and Hángzhōu 杭州 became the most important waterway connecting northern and southern China. After the completion of the railroad between Jǐnán and Qīngdǎo 青岛 at the end of the 19th century and the opening of Jǐnán to foreign trade by the Qīng 清 (1616 - 1911) Court in 1906, the city became a thriving business center as well as a prominent political center. In 1929, the city of Jǐnán was officially established.

Jǐnán is home to many historical figures. The list of figures is seemingly endless, including Biǎn Què 扁鹊 (the

Gong Li (b. 1965), a Jinan native, is recognized worldwide for her starring roles in many of Zhang Yimou's films such as "Red Sorghum," "Raise the Red Lantern," "The Story of Qiu Ju," and "Curse of the Golden Flower." In recent years, she also took up roles in Hollywood films including "Memoirs of a Geisha," "Chinese Box," "Miami Vice," and "Hannibal Rising."

first doctor of traditional Chinese medicine), Zōu Yǎn 邹衍, (founder of the Yīn 阴 and Yáng 阳 Five Element School), and Lǐ Qīngzhào 李清照 and Xīn Qìjī 辛弃疾 (two of the most established Cí 词 poets of the Sòng 宋 Dyansty). Gǒng Lì 巩俐, a contemporary Chinese film actress, is also a native of Jǐnán. What is it about Jǐnán that allowed so many prominent figures to emerge? Was it its geographic location, its beautiful misty mountains, its flowing springs and rivers, its peaceful lakes, the influence of Confucian principles, the thriving foreign trade and the presence of so many Buddhist temples and figures? Whatever the reasons, visitors will no doubt want to return to this place.

Highlights

In ancient times, Jǐnán was full of natural water springs. In fact, Jǐnán was nicknamed the "City of Springs" or quán chéng 泉城. It has been recorded that the city's old area alone had over 140 springs. Though most of the springs are dry now, the others, namely Bàotū 趵突 Spring (Spurting Spring), Hēihǔ 黑虎 (Black Tiger) Spring, Zhēnzhū 珍珠 (Pearl) Spring, and Wǔlóng 五龙 (Five Dragon) Spring are still active. In the old days, each household had a spring running through its property, graced by weeping willows. This made Jǐnán more like a southern Chinese city. Today, this old and picturesque Jǐnán can still be found in the center of the city. The old architectural stores, civilian residences, and the Fúróng 芙蓉 (Lotus) Street are all testimonies to the prosperity and elegance of the city's past. To the northeast of the old city is Dàmíng Hú 大明湖 (Lake), another famous scenic spot in Jǐnán, covering an area of 46 hectares. A natural lake, Dàmíng Hú is also associated with the lotus flower. Since the Táng Dynasty, lotus have been planted in the lake, and on June 24th of each lunar calendar, people row boats in the lake and light lotus lanterns as a gesture to celebrate life and living.

During the Suí Dynasty, some Buddhist carvings were completed in the cliffs and a Thousand-Buddha Temple was built on the Thousand-Buddha Mountain or Qiānfó Shān 千佛山. Though the mountain is only about 300 metres high, from its peak, you can get a panoramic view of the city. Another Buddhist presence is the colorful sculptures at the Língyán 灵岩 Temple. Carved in the Sòng Dynasty, these 40 arhat clay sculptures are considered the best in China.

Food

While in Jǐnán, don't miss the chance to enjoy some snacks made from lotus such as fried lotus, lotus leaf congee, crystal lotus root, and candied lotus seeds. The Milked Púcài 蒲菜 Soup of Jǐnán called nǎi tāng púcài 奶汤蒲菜 is also worth mentioning as it's considered the best soup in Jǐnán. It's made of milk and púcài, a vegetable only available from the Dàmíng Lake. The soup is creamy and has a very delicate taste, but the púcài is crisp.

The Green City

A Ring Park with beautiful old trees and vegetation surrounds the city of Jǐnán. It covers an area of 26.3 hectares,

To the northeast of the old city is Daming Hu (Lake), a large natural lake where many lotus flowers grow. It's a nice place for a stroll.

Jinan policemen have a reputation for being polite while on duty, which is considered uncommon in China.

In the southwest part of Jinan is Thousand Buddha Mountain or Qianfo Shan, a destination to see Buddhist statues that were carved during the Sui Dynasty (581 - 618 C.E.).

Fast Facts

Formal Name: Jǐnán 济南

AKA: City of Springs

Symbols:
Flower: Lotus or héhuā 荷花
Tree: Willow or liǔshù 柳树

Land Size: 8,177 sq km

Population: 5.96 million

Famous For:
The springs, Dàmíng Lake, clay Buddhist sculptures at the Língyán Temple, Lǐ Qīngzhào's Residence, Black Pottery, and Milked Púcài Soup

Explore-A-Province in China®

Historically known for its many natural springs, Jinan looks more like a southern Chinese city than a northern one.

and stretches 4.71 km long, and is studded with springs and lakes. The Ring Park is something the locals treasure. Taking a walk there is always a pleasure. Along with the ring parks in Héféi 合肥, Ānhuī 安徽 Province and in Xī'ān 西安, Shaanxi Province, the Ring Park in Jǐnán is considered to be one of the best in the country.

Industries and Future Development

Jǐnán, the city of ancient civilizations and culture, has recently opened itself to scientific and technological innovations. The municipal government has put an emphasis on building infrastructure to create new industrial opportunities. Jǐnán has also developed into a major technology center for software exports.

A bird's-eye view of the Wulong (Five Dragon) Spring.

Shandong City Life

Qingdao

Location: Southern coast of Shāndōng 山东
Population: 7.4 million
Size: 11,026 sq km (4,256 sq miles)

With red-roofed German-style houses, green trees, and long beaches, Qīngdǎo 青岛, the nation's fourth largest port, is a perfect summer resort. Many of the houses were built during the late 19th century by Germans who once colonized Qīngdǎo. The city was then occupied by the Japanese in the early 20th century. The city, then, has a somewhat foreign look, both European and Asian. Among the many attractions of Qīngdǎo, Láoshān 崂山, a Daoist mountain, is a must-see. Stop by a tea farm or the Huádōng 华东 Winery. While in Qīngdǎo, don't forget to take a break to taste the locally produced but globally distributed Tsingtsao (Qīngdǎo) Beer.

The Jinan Colloquial Language

Like many people in Shāndōng 山东, Jǐnán 济南 locals like to add the sound of zǐ 子 after a certain person or a certain object, i.e. Kǒng Zǐ 孔子, Sūn Zǐ 孙子, Mèng Zǐ 孟子, jīzǐ 鸡子 for jīdàn 鸡蛋 (egg), bàngzǐ 棒子 for yùmǐ 玉米 (corn), bèizǐ 被子 for miánbèi 棉被 (quilt) and chēzǐ 车子 for chē 车 (car or bicycle). Usually when they speak these words, an "er" sound accompanies the sound of "zi."

Another interesting thing one notices in Jǐnán is the way people address each other. Many, especially those over the age of 40, will say, "Good morning, Teacher Lǐ 李" or "Teacher Zhāng 张, are you feeling better these days?" Hearing this frequent use of "teacher," visitors might think that there must be many teachers in Shāndōng. Actually, not everyone addressed in this manner is a teacher or lǎoshī 老师. To refer to someone as teacher, and not as Mr., Ms., comrade or tóngzhì 同志, Lǎo 老 (senior) or Xiǎo 小 (junior), is very common in Jǐnán. This reverential form of address is a remnant of the deep influence of Confucianism on Shāndōng. Confucius is regarded as the greatest teacher in Chinese history. During his lifetime, he talked a great deal about the utmost reverence one needs to show to teachers.

Jinan has an older generation of well-educated and sophisticated residents who live not far from the birthplace of Confucius. This famous philosopher emphasized throughout his lifetime the importance of education.

Yantai

Location: Northeast tip of the Shāndōng Peninsula
Population: 6.48 million
Size: 13,748 sq km (5,307 sq miles)

A beautiful coastal city bordering the Yellow Sea or Huánghǎi 黄海 and the Bó Sea or Bóhǎi 渤海, Yāntái 烟台 sits in a very strategic position. It faces Dàlián 大连 of Liáoníng 辽宁 Province to the north, and South Korea and Japan to the east. Yāntái and the surrounding area, with its sea breezes and warm climate, abound in fruits

Yantai

22

including apples, pears, grape and Chinese chestnuts. Yāntái is known as the City of Wine, with vineyards stretching for miles. The city also has a century-long history of piano production. Shāndōng cuisine actually originated in Yāntái.

WEIHAI
Location: Very eastern tip of Shāndōng Peninsula
Population: 2.5 million
Size: 5,436 sq km (2,098 sq miles)

The earliest place in China to see the sunrise, Wēihǎi 威海 City has special charms: mountains, sea, islands, beaches, springs, forests, and historic places. Honored as the first "National Environmental City" in China, Wēihǎi has a very enjoyable climate; the winters aren't too cold, and the summers aren't too hot. Backed by mountains and facing the sea, Wēihǎi has turned into an ideal place for tourists. Abundant aquatic resources have also made Wēihǎi one of the largest fish production bases in China.

JINING
Location: Southwest Shāndōng
Population: 8.05 million
Size: 11,286 sq km (4,356 sq miles)

Qūfǔ 曲阜 is the hometown of Confucius and Mencius hails from Zōuchéng 邹城. The two cities are both under Jǐníng's 济宁 administration. Every year over 5.5 million visitors come to Qūfǔ to see the three Kongs: the Mansion of Confucius or Kǒngfǔ 孔府; the Temple of Confucius or Kǒngmiào 孔庙; and the Confucian Cemetery or Kǒnglín 孔林. The three sites were designated a UNESCO World Cultural Heritage Site. While there, don't miss the Confucian Banquet, one of the most refined meals in China.

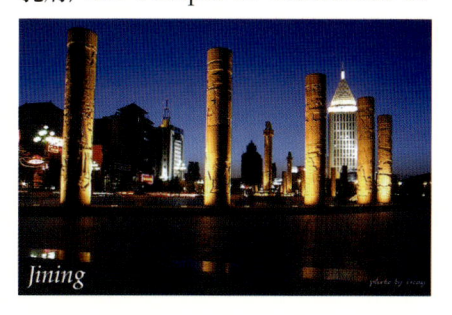

WEIFANG
Location: Central Shāndōng between Jǐnán 济南 and Qīngdǎo
Population: 8.53 million
Size: 15,770 sq km (6,087 sq miles)

For those interested in China's ancient history and folk art, Wéifāng 潍坊 should be at the top of the list. As a 7,000-year-old city, it's full of cultural relics. Qīngzhōu 青州 (a city under Wéifāng's administration) has a large collection of Buddhist statues from the Southern and Northern Dynasties (420 - 589 C.E.). Wéifāng is known as the Kite Capital of the World, hosting the Wéifāng International Kite Festival each April and housing the International Kite Museum. Wéifāng is still active today in making and trading kites. New year woodblock prints, papercuts, and clay toys made by farmers there are collectible items for lovers of folk art. A region in Wéifāng called Shòuguāng 寿光 is also a major vegetable production and distribution base in China.

ZIBO
Location: Center of Shāndōng Province
Population: 4.17 million
Size: 5,939 sq km (2,293 sq miles)

Zībó 淄博 was the capital of the State of Qí 齐 in the Spring and Autumn Period (770 - 476 B.C.E.) and the Warring States Period (475 - 221 B.C.E.). The excavated pits of chariots and horses buried 2,500 years ago tell that the city was very well-developed. Zībó used to be a production center for ceramics and silk weaving, and served as one of the starting points of the Silk Road after the Hàn 汉 Dynasty (206 B.C.E. - 220 C.E.).

DEZHOU
Location: Northwest Shāndōng
Population: 5.52 million
Size: 10,356 sq km (3,997 sq miles)

Dézhōu 德州 sits among Běijīng 北京, Tiānjīn 天津, and Shíjiāzhuāng 石家庄, the capital of Héběi 河北 Province, and has been an important wharf along the Great Běijīng-Hángzhōu 北京－杭州 Canal. Because of this strategic position, the city has been a transportation hub in northern China. The famous "three treasures of Dézhōu" include Dézhōu braised chickens, Dézhōu watermelons and Lèlíng 乐陵 dates.

HEZE
Location: Southwest Shāndōng, bordering Hénán 河南 and Ānhuī 安徽 provinces
Population: 8.88 million
Size: 12,238 sq km (4,724 sq miles)

Visitors come to Hézé 菏泽 primarily for one thing, the peony, the national flower of China. The city exports 70% of the country's peonies. The history of growing peonies dates back to even before the Qín 秦 Dynasty (221 - 206 B.C.E.). The soil and the climate there are especially suitable for growing peonies. Every year in May, when peonies are in bloom, the city holds the Hézé International Peony Festival.

Provincial People

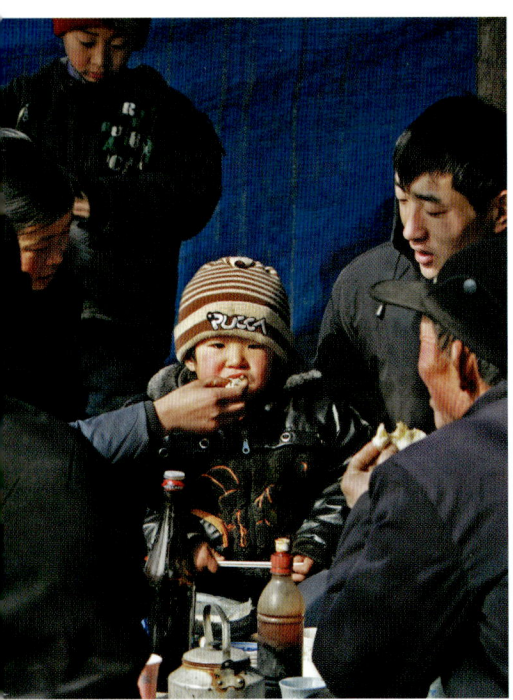

An Oral Portrait

Grandma and grandson turning a millstone. They live in a small village in the mountains of western Shandong.

Grandma feeding her grandson. In rural Shandong, a boy carries the family's hopes for the future, so the child is well taken care of even after he gets married.

One evening while in Jǐnán 济南, the capital of Shāndōng 山东 Province, Emma was invited by Xiǎo Mèng 小孟, her tour guide, to dine in a small restaurant in one of the old lanes. Like most Chinese cities, Jǐnán is under demolition. Old districts full of the traditional one-level family houses are being leveled, as the ground is being excavated to prepare for high-rises. The dinner table was soon full of small and exotic dishes that Emma would never have dreamt of ordering, and she was surrounded by local people who love to dine out. Emma bombarded Xiǎo Mèng with questions concerning the people of Shāndōng. Here was how Xiǎo Mèng presented the Shāndōng people:

According to the many researchers at home and abroad who specialize in anthropology, there is a consensus that Shāndōng people best exemplify those in northern China. They are very distinctive in appearance; they are usually tall, well-built, and have attractive chiseled features. A certain scholar by the name of Zhāng Tiānlín 张天麟 holds that Shāndōng people are like the first sons of the Chinese nation; their good qualities stand out. They are known to be responsible but a bit reserved, hard-working but a bit stubborn, and doers rather than talkers.

Shāndōng is the birthplace of Confucius or Kǒng Zǐ 孔子 (551 - 479 B.C.E.). The impact of his teachings known as Confucianism, combined with the teachings of Mencius or Mèng Zǐ 孟子 (372-289 B.C.E.), another Shāndōng native, is immeasurable. Two examples best attest to the immense impact these thinkers had on Shāndōng people, and by extension on others in China who adopted Confucianism. The province has had the lowest crime rate and divorce rate for many years. What do these statistics have to do with Confucianism? As true believers of this orthodox teaching, the people live on Confucian principles such as benevolence, virtue, honesty, and loyalty. Consequently, they represent the ideal human being and ideal citizen. As individuals they love, respect, and protect their families, and they hold their relationships within their family sacred, never abandoning them for any reason. Shāndōng people are brought up to be law-abiding citizens.

One aspect of Confucianism especially appreciated and practiced in Shāndōng is filial piety or xiàodào 孝道. To many, not being filial towards one's parents is considered almost as serious as a crime. In Shāndōng, filial devotion is seen as important in a marriage. Filial piety and obedience are reflected in the way Shāndōng people work and live. Often they are good listeners and follow instructions well, but they are not leaders or innovators.

Shāndōng people are known for being frugal. They would rather save than spend. As one Chinese saying goes, "The people in Shāndōng like to store grains whereas those in Shānxī 山西 like to build houses." It's said that in Shāndōng, most mothers look for one quality in their prospective daughter-in-laws: the ability to manage a family on a budget and help her husband get rich through saving.

Throughout the country, Shāndōng people are also reputed to be very open and straightforward. They are described as having a mouth as sharp as a knife but a heart as soft as dòufu 豆腐 (tofu). Once they regard someone as a friend worthy of trust, they're very devoted, just like the unforgettable characters in the famous novel *The Outlaws of the Marsh*. This novel is valued for many reasons, but mostly because it reflects the true character of Shāndōng people.

With the help of the government's Hope Project, village girls in Shandong can now finish high school education. Across China, Hope Schools are set up to assist rural children from poor families with their studies. Though set up by China Youth Development Foundation, a quasi-government organization, funds are raised from people from all walks of life and institutions of various kinds.

Common Surnames in Shandong

孔 Kǒng
Location: Mostly in Qūfǔ 曲阜
Descendants of Confucius or Kǒng Zǐ 孔子

孟 Mèng
Location: Mostly in Zōuchéng 邹城, Qūfǔ
Descendants of Qìngfù 庆父 in the Spring and Autumn Period (Mencius was a famous descendant)

邹 Zōu
Location: Mostly in Zōuchéng, Qūfǔ
Descendants of (1) son of King Zhōu 周 of the Shāng 商 Dynasty and (2) a tribe led by Chī Yóu 蚩尤 before the Xià 夏 Dynasty

姜 Jiāng
Location: Mostly in Línzī 临淄, Zībó 淄博
Descendants of (1) Shén Nóng 神农 (the god of farming, said to have lived around 2800 B.C.E.) and (2) Jiāng Tàigōng 姜太公 or Jiāng Zǐyá 姜子牙, the founding father of the State of Qí 齐 during the Spring and Autumn Period

孙 Sūn
Location: Mostly in Guǎngráo 广饶 County, Zībó 淄博
Descendants of Sūn Zǐ 孙子, author of *The Art of War*

董 Dǒng
Location: Mostly in Dìngtáo 定陶 County, Jǐníng 济宁
Descendants of Huáng Dì 黄帝 (the Yellow Emperor)

曹 Cáo
Location: Mostly in Dìngtáo County, Jǐníng
Descendants of (1) a grandson of Huáng Dì (the Yellow Emperor) named Zhuān Xū 颛顼 and (2) a brother of King Zhōu Wǔ 周武

曾 Zēng
Location: Mostly in Cāngshān 苍山 County, Línyí 临沂
Descendants of the King Yǔ 禹 of the Xià 夏 Dynasty

丁 Dīng
Location: Mostly in Zībó 淄博
Descendants of a son of Jiāng Tàigōng or Jiāng Zǐyá

薛 Xuē
Location: Mostly in Téngzhōu 滕州
Descendants of (1) the last son of Huáng Dì (the Yellow Emperor) and (2) Tián Yīng 田婴, father of Mèngcháng Jūn 孟尝君 of the Warring States Period

任 Rén
Location: Mostly in Jǐníng
Descendants of (1) Fú Xī 伏羲, inventor of the Eight Diagrams and (2) a son of Huáng Dì, the Yellow Emperor

姚 Yáo
Location: Mostly in Juànchéng 鄄城 County, Hézé 菏泽
Descendants of King Shùn 舜

谭 Tán
Location: Mostly in Zhāngqiū 章丘
Descendants of King Yǔ 禹, the legendary conqueror of floods

金 Jīn
Location: Mostly in Qūfǔ, Jǐníng
Descendants of the famous leader of the Dōng Yí 东夷 Tribe named Shào Hào 少昊

崔 Cuī
Location: Mostly in Zhāngqiū
Descendants of Jiāng Tàigōng or Jiāng Zǐyá

邱 Qiū
Location: Mostly in Zībó
Descendants of Jiāng Tàigōng or Jiāng Zǐyá

陆 Lù
Location: Mostly in Jǐnán 济南
Descendants of Jiāng Tàigōng or Jiāng Zǐyá

A Shandong Couple's Dream

Married for over 40 years, Gài Jìngdé 盖敬德 and Zhāng Xiùlán 张秀兰 in Huìmín 惠民 County are compatible in many ways. They are together almost every minute of the day, working in the fields, cooking and eating together, and thinking of their only daughter who is a migrant worker in Běijīng 北京.

Unlike most other older farmers in rural China whose spare time is mostly spent taking care of grandchildren and playing mahjong, this couple takes great pleasure in making paper cuts. The husband, Gài Jìngdé, a born artist, can draw anything he sees, while his wife, Zhāng Xiùlán can turn any design of her husband's into a paper cut. Soon after she was married, Zhāng Xiùlán got the nickname qiǎoshǒu 巧手, meaning someone very skilled working with one's hands. The couple has been collaborating on paper cuts for half a century. In 2008, their favorite theme was the Běijīng Olympics. By cutting the five mascots called fúwá 福娃, they felt closer to their beloved daughter and to the country's capital that they've always dreamt of visiting.

Shandong Profile

Husband and wife going to a fair in a coastal village. In this part of eastern Shandong, farmers and fishermen normally cover their houses with a kind of seaweed that can keep houses warm in winter and cool in summer.

(above) A woman in Ju County, Shandong, is presenting a wonderful display of beautifully made buns known as dough figures. These wheat products are popular in northern China where wheat is the main crop. Dough figures are made for special occasions such as weddings, funerals, birthdays, festivals, and ancestral worship.

(left) During a Chinese wedding ceremony, newlyweds bow to their parents as a gesture of gratitude for their many years of upbringing.

(below) People practice taiji quan in the picturesque city of Qingdao.

Explore-A-Province in China®

Philosophical Roots

Shāndōng 山东 is closely linked with "China's Golden Age," a period known as the "Hundred Schools of Thought" throughout the Spring and Autumn (770 - 476 B.C.E.) and the Warring States periods (475 - 221 B.C.E). The time was particularly prolific for arts, sciences and humanities.

Mo Zi, founder of Mohism, was respected by the lower class throughout Chinese history.

Mohism

During the Warring States Period in Chinese history, there was a movement that propagated the notion of "Universal Love." Its founder, chief proponent, and a major contributor to China's philosophical development was a man named Mò Zǐ 墨子 (476 - 390 B.C.E.).

Mò Zǐ, born in Téngzhōu 滕州, Shāndōng 山东, came from a laboring family. His ideas represented the most substantial opposition to the very traditional beliefs of Confucius. His philosophy was non-violent and held that compassion and empathy should be shared and expressed equally among all members of society, irrespective of the rank, lineage or age. His first-hand experience of the misery of war convinced him that "Universal Love" was the key to peace and stability. He was frugal and rejected excess of any kind, including elaborate funeral rites. This directly contradicted the Confucian call for burial rites that reflected the societal position of the deceased. Mò Zǐ was also an inventor and friend to Lǔ Bān 鲁班, another prominent inventor at the time. The two men shared the belief that their designs should enhance the common good. Mò Zǐ's writing was complied into a book known as *Mò Zǐ* by some of his followers. His school of thought in Chinese philosophy became known as Mohism.

The Military School of Philosophy

Among the "Hundred Schools of Thought" that flourished during the Spring and Autumn Period, the military school of philosophy exerted a great influence on Chinese history. Thinkers devoted to the military strategies were often referred to as bīngjiā 兵家. Sūn Zǐ 孙子 remains the most influential of these thinkers. His signature piece, *The Art of War* or Sūn Zǐ Bīngfǎ 孙子兵法, composed roughly 2,500 years ago, continues to remain relevant.

If you know your enemies and know yourself, you will win a hundred times in a hundred battles.
Zhī jǐ zhī bǐ, bǎi zhàn bú dài
知已知彼，百战不殆。

This idiom, attributed to Sūn Zǐ, is one of many wonderful and insightful collections of battlefield assessments; of weakness, strength, advantage, and disadvantage. Sūn Zǐ lived around the same period as Confucius (551 - 479 B.C.E.), a period when wars were nearly constant; 300 wars in a 150 year period. The constant fighting during the Warring States Period provided military strategists with ample opportunity to develop and refine their strategies and executions.

Though *The Art of War* reveals little of the writer Sūn Zǐ, it is known that he was born into a respected military

In 1972, a large number of bamboo strips were unearthed by chance from a Western Han (206 B.C.E. - 25 C.E.) tomb at Silver Sparrow Mountain, Linyi County, Shandong. Among the strips were some chapters of Sun Zi's "The Art of War." The archeological find proved that Sun Zi did exist.

Wu: an Anti-war Chinese Character

Interestingly enough, the Chinese character for war or "martial" (wǔ 武) consists of two characters, gē 戈, the most popular long weapon used in ancient times, and zhǐ 止, meaning to stop. The original meaning of wǔ in Chinese is to stop using of military weapons. Here, an important martial arts idea is best conveyed in the formation of the character. Martial arts are not for fighting, but to stop fighting.

28

The way that terracotta warriors in the tomb of Qin Shihuang were lined up is actually a product of studies of military formations in "The Art of War."

have been handed down through history. These chapters cover many aspects related to warfare. Sūn Zǐ was a pioneer in military theory, introducing important ideas such as the "indirect approach," moral consideration, and psychology. One of his famous ideas is that "Seizing the enemy without fighting is the most skillful."

Some of Máo Zédōng's 毛泽东 (1893 - 1976) military strategies were derived and developed from the theories of Sūn Zǐ. During the Vietnam War, the North Vietnamese officers, many of whom could actually recite the book, exercised these theories. Today, the book is studied by diplomats, politicians, business persons, and by those wanting to learn more about tactical engagement.

family in the State of Qí 齐 (part of today's Shāndōng Province) and spent most of his life in the State of Wú 吴 (today's Jiāngsū 江苏 Province) as a military consultant to the King of Wú.

Thirteen chapters of his original book

Sūn Zǐ 孙子
(Dates unknown. He lived around the same time as Confucius.)

AKA: Sūn Wǔ 孙武, Sūn Chángqīng 孙长卿
From: Guǎngráo 广饶, Shāndōng 山东
Known For: Author of *The Art of War*, one of the worlds' earliest collections of military strategy, doctrine and related tactics.

Sūn Zǐ was born to an aristocratic and military family in the State of Qí 齐 (present-day Shāndōng Province). When wars broke out in the country, he fled to the State of Wú 吴 (present-day Jiāngsū 江苏 Province) and became a primary military consultant to the king of the State of Wú until his death.

Sūn Zǐ's book is a thorough collection of wisdoms, idioms and even instructions on how to defeat the enemy without engaging him in warfare directly. By the Táng 唐 Dynasty (618 - 907 C.E.), the book had made its way to Japan. In the 18th century, the book made its way to Europe and finally to America. It has been said that Napoleon, upon his defeat, had regretted not having consulted the book at an earlier stage in his military campaigns.

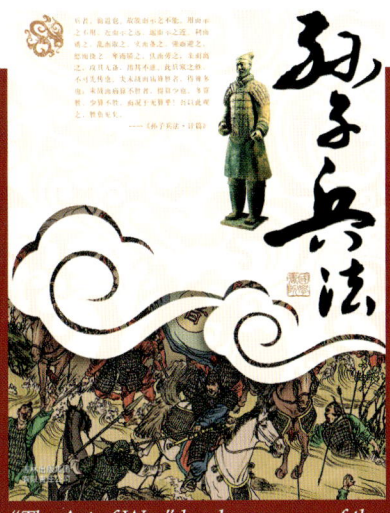

"The Art of War" has become one of the best known military books of all time. Today, it is read by people in many different cultures and countries.

Sun Zi: Turning Concubines into Warriors

Legend says that before the king of the State of Wú 吴 hired Sūn Zǐ 孙子 to work for him, the king tested him by giving him 180 of his concubines to be trained as battle-ready soldiers. Sūn Zǐ first divided the women into two groups and appointed two of the king's favorites as group commanders. He then asked the women to distinguish between left and right, forward and backward, and also explained the importance of obeying orders. Afterwards, the drum signaled a right turn, but all of the women stood there and laughed. Sūn Zǐ apologized to the ladies for his unclear directions. Once again, he patiently explained the exercise, and the drums sounded.

The women laughed again and no one moved. To everyone's astonishment, Sūn Zǐ ordered the two group leaders executed, refusing to repeal the order even at the king's request. He explained that, as a general, he was bound to act with a general's authority. Sūn Zǐ continued his training, and soon the women were trained to be formidable warriors.

Explore-A-Province in China®

Ci poetry had its own melody and lyrics and was easier to compose than Tang Shi.

The Written World

Shāndōng 山东 has a rich literary legacy. From Cí 词 poetry to Chinese classic novels, let's get a glimpse of the achievements of some great writers and poets from Shāndōng.

Cí Poetry

Cí 词 poetry rose from the musings of ordinary people of the Táng 唐 Dynasty 618 - 907 C.E.), a period of prolificacy and prosperity in Chinese history. Cí literally means "words to a tune" with each Cí having its own melody and lyrics. Compared to Táng Shī 唐诗 (poems) prevalent at the time, Cí was literal, giving more freedom to express emotions and was also easier to compose.

It was in the Sòng 宋 Dynasty (960 - 1279 C.E.) that the Cí poetry went into full development. Among the most accomplished Cí poets in the Sòng Dynasty were Lǐ Qīngzhào 李清照 and Xīn Qìjí 辛弃疾. Though both of them were natives of Shāndōng 山东, their Cí styles are remarkably different. Lǐ Qīngzhào's poems, more in line with the school of Wēn Tíngyùn 温庭蕴 and Lǐ Yù 李煜, are more subtle and explicit. Xīn Qìjí's, on the other hand, follow Sū Shì's 苏轼 school, and are more free and powerful.

A Ci Poem by Li Qingzhao

Seeking, Seeking Shēngshēngmàn
声声慢

Seeking, seeking,
xún xún mì mì
寻寻觅觅

Chilly and quiet,
lěng lěng qīng qīng
冷冷清清,

Desolate, painful and miserable.
qī qī cǎn cǎn qī qī
凄凄惨惨戚戚。

Even when it's warmer there is still a chill,
zhà nuǎn hái hán shí hòu
乍暖还寒时候,

It is most difficult to keep well.
zuì nán jiāng xī
最难将息

Three or two cups of light wine,
sān bēi liǎng zhǎn dàn jiǔ
三杯两盏淡酒,

How can they ward off the strong morning wind?
zěn dí tā, wǎn lái fēng jí
怎敌它,晚来风急?

30

Wild geese fly past, while I'm broken hearted;
yàn guò yě, zhèng shāng xīn
雁过也，正伤心，

But I recognize they are my old friends.
què shì jiù shí xiāng shí
却是旧时相识。

Fallen chrysanthemums piled up on the ground,
mǎn dì huáng huā duī jī
满地黄花堆积，

So withered,
qiáo cuì sǔn
憔悴损

Who would pluck them?
rú jīn yǒu shuí kān zhāi
如今有谁堪摘？

Leaning on the window,
shǒu zhe chuāng'er
守着窗儿，

How can I pass the time 'till night alone?
dū zì zěn shēng de hēi
独自怎生得黑？

The drizzle falls on the wutong (Chinese parasol) trees,
wú tóng gèng jiān xì yǔ
梧桐更兼细雨，

Rain drops drip down at dusk.
dào huáng hūn, diǎn diǎn dī dī
到黄昏，点点滴滴。

At a time like this,
zhè cì dì
这次第，

What immense sorrow I must bear!
zěn yī gè chóu zì liǎo de
怎一个愁字了得！

(Translated by Lǐ Zǐliàng 李子亮, Lǐ Guóqìng 李国庆, and Zhào Fēifēi 赵菲菲)

A painting by Sha Fu, a late Qing Dynasty artist. It's widely acknowledged that his paintings of young Chinese ladies reflect the sentiment of sorrow.

Lǐ Qīngzhào 李清照 (1084 - 1151 C.E.)

AKA: Lǐ Yì'ān 李易安, Yì'ān Jūshì 易安居士
From: Jǐnán 济南, Shāndōng 山东
Known for: Being one of the best female poets pre-20th century

Unlike most women from ancient times who couldn't read and write, Lǐ Qīngzhào received a very good education from her parents, who were both intellectuals. From an early age, she demonstrated great talent in composing poems in the cí 词 style. In 1101 C.E., she married Zhào Míngchéng 赵明诚, a young and promising imperial scholar who had a deep love for collecting ancient books, scrolls, and curios. The early days in their marriage were idyllic; the couple was so compatible with each other both in taste and literary writing. But their lives were shattered by the Jurchen invasion from the north. The Jurchens defeated the Northern Sòng 宋 Dynasty (960 - 1127 C.E.), forcing the Sòng emperor to flee south. During this chaos, Zhào Míngchéng contracted an illness and died in 1129 C.E. Having lost both the man and much of their invaluable collection, Lǐ Qīngzhào moved to the south and settled down in Hángzhōu 杭州, where she lived out her days by writing sorrowful Cí poetry.

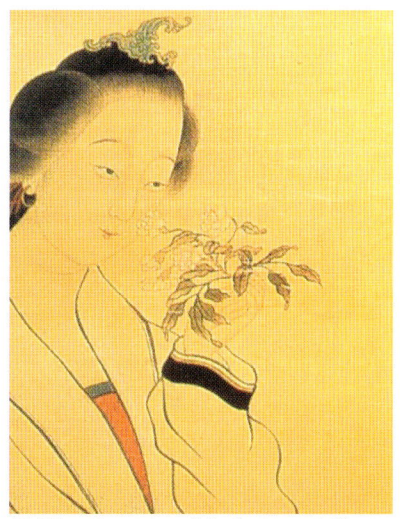

Li Qingzhao, one of the best pre-20th century female poets

Though a military general, Xin Qiji is best remembered today as a warrior poet.

Xīn Qìjí 辛弃疾 (1140 - 1207 C.E.)

AKA: Xīn Jiàxuān 辛稼轩
From: Jǐnán 济南, Shāndōng 山东
Known for: Heroic Cí style poems and his contribution against the Jurchen invaders

Out of the 620 Cí poems by Xīn Qìjí, most of them are lyrics about the man's ambitions to gain back lost territories invaded by the Jurchen tribes from the north. This won him the title of a warrior poet. Because the top rulers of the Southern Sòng 宋 Dynasty (1127 - 1279 C.E.) were too timid to fight the invaders, he eventually became discontent. Though he was a military general, he is best remembered today as a poet, because he combined various styles of prose and even put folk idioms into his Cí poems, broadening the genre with themes and expressions prevalent at the time.

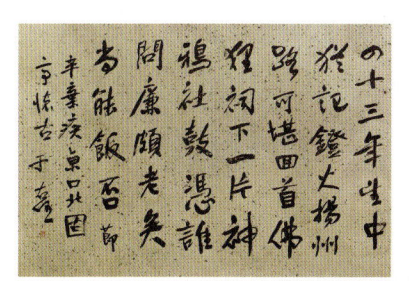

A copy of Xin Qiji's Ci poem by famed Chinese calligrapher Yu Youren

OUTLAWS OF THE MARSH

Outlaws of the Marsh or Shuǐ Hǔ Zhuàn 水浒传 is one of the four great classics in Chinese literature. It is about a group of peasant heroes (105 men and three women) who live as bandits outside normal society. Stories about these heroes were already popular in the Sòng 宋 Dynasty (960 - 1279 C.E.). At that time, most stories were written as scripts that were read aloud by storytellers in teahouses rather than as novels read silently to oneself. Scripts written down this way were called huàběn 话本, literally meaning "storyteller's script." Huàběn was the basic form of folk literature during the Sòng and Yuán 元 (1206 - 1368) dynasties.

The standarized version of the novel about Sòng Jiāng 宋江, the central hero, and his fellow men is the outcome of the work of Shī Nài'ān 施耐庵 (1296 - 1371), who lived in the 14th century. In his depiction of the bandits who supposedly lived at Liángshānpō 梁山泊, Jǐníng 济宁, Shāndōng 山东, Shī Nài'ān creates a utopian universe outside the "civilized" world, emphasizing the bandits' heroic qualities. In one passage, for example, he writes that these bandits fear "neither heaven, earth nor the court, sharing gold and silver together and clad in rare silk, eat meat and drink wine to their fill."

An interesting twist in this novel has to do with the bandits' attitude towards the reigning emperor. Although they live as outsiders and fight bitterly against the corrupt officials, avaricious merchants, and oppressive landlords, they nevertheless believe in the right of the emperor to reign over the people. Their belief in the emperor sets their skirmishes and uprisings apart from many fundamentally subversive uprisings in Chinese history. Their identity outside of society and their faithfulness to the emperor bring these bandits into problematic situations and to a tragic end.

Colorful characterization and suspenseful storytelling have made *Outlaws of the March* the classic that it is

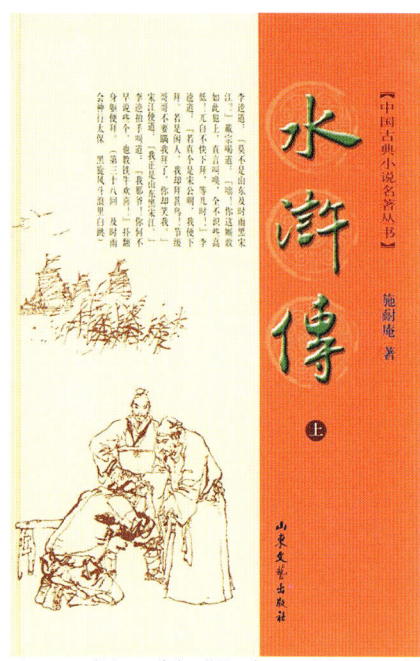

A new edition of the "Outlaws of the Marsh"

today. After attracting people's imagination for centuries in China, several English translations were made, allowing the novel to reach a broader readership outside China. These translations include Sidney Shapiro's *Outlaws of the Marsh* and Pearl Buck's *All Men are Brothers*.

An old woodblock picture from Yangliuqing, Tianjin. The main characters in "Outlaws of the Marsh" are gathered in front of The Hall of Faith and Right.

The bandits in the *Outlaws of the Marsh* are loved not only for their bravery and intelligence, but also for their mastery of Chinese martial arts. Many of them are good at using a certain Chinese weapon. The weapons they used in the novel are collectively called the "Eighteen Military Weapons or shíbā bān wǔyì 十八般武艺." The term, already popular in the Sòng 宋 Dynasty (960 - 1279 C.E.), generally refers to the weapons as shown on this page (sketches by Chinese artist Dài Dūnbāng 戴敦邦). Today, the usage of this term has broadened to describe a person's versatility.

Axe (Fǔ 斧)

Bow (Gōng 弓)

Dagger (Bì 匕)

Dagger axe (Gē 戈)

Fork (Chā 叉)

Halberd (Jǐ 戟)

Lance (Máo 矛)

Long stick axe (Yuè 钺)

Meteor hammer (Chuí 锤)

Monk cudgel (Zhàng 杖)

Sabre (Dāo 刀)

Shield (Pái 牌)

Shovel (Qiāo 锹)

Spear (Qiāng 枪)

Staff (Gùn 棍)

Steel whip (Biān 鞭)

Straight sword (Jiàn 剑)

Wolf teeth club (Bàng 棒)

"Court Ladies of the Former Shu," a painting by Tang Yin (1470 - 1523). Tang Yin was a famous Ming Dynasty painter, poet, and calligrapher. A large part of his fame came from his vivid drawing of women.

A page in the "The Plum in the Golden Vase." As the first Chinese vernacular novel, it has influenced many Chinese novels including "A Dream of Red Mansions."

The Plum in the Golden Vase

Western readers might have heard of the four great classical Chinese novels: *Romance of the Three Kingdoms*, *Journey to the West*, *Outlaws of the Marsh*, and *A Dream of Red Mansions*. Few, however, know that *A Dream of Red Mansions* was not originally included on this list. Before the famed *A Dream of Red Mansions*, another novel, *The Plum in the Golden Vase* or Jīn Píng Méi 金瓶梅, stood in its place. But during the Qīng 清 Dynasty (1616 - 1911), this novel was banned as pornographic and replaced.

The Plum in the Golden Vase came out during the reign of Míng 明 Dynasty Emperor Wàn Lì 万历 (1572 - 1619). The author published the novel under the pseudonym Lánlíng Xiào Xiào Shēng 兰陵笑笑生, which literally means a laughing guy from Lánlíng 兰陵 (present day Zǎozhuāng 枣庄 City, Shāndōng 山东). The novel is set in the Northern Sòng 宋 Dynasty (960 - 1127 C.E.), following a plot thread in *Outlaws of the Marsh*. Instead of centering on the bandits and their heroism, however, *The Plum in the Golden Vase* centers on the domestic life of Xīmén Qìng 西门庆, a wealthy but corrupt merchant with six wives and concubines. Through his conspicuous consumption, political corruption, and excessive sex, Xīmén Qìng follows a path that brings harm to others and destruction to himself. In his description of Xīmén Qìng and the society that surrounds him, the author comments on 16th century society — a time of tight political control at the top, corruption at various levels, and the gradual degradation of traditional values.

The Míng Dynasty saw a rise of popular literature and erotic art, thanks to the nationwide spread of woodblock printing techniques. Actually, *The Plum in the Golden Vase* was the first Chinese vernacular novel that was written by a single novelist, serving as a model for many later vernacular novels, such as *A Dream of Red Mansions*.

Strange Tales from Make-Do Studio

Early Chinese history is interwoven with fairy tales and fantasies. It is believed that Nǚ Wā 女娲, the woman who supposedly created the Chinese nation, had a human head and a snake body. Legend also tells that Yǔ 禹, the legendary conqueror of great floods, married a nine-tailed fox. Female figures in Chinese myths and fantasies are often emblems of beauty and wisdom and take the form of animals.

Centuries after these fairy tales and fantasies were first told, other stories sharing similar qualities were put together into a collection called *Strange Tales from Make-Do Studio* or Liáo Zhāi Zhì Yì 聊斋志异. The 17th century book incorporated styles prevalent in Táng 唐 Dynasty (618 - 907 C.E.) romances or chuánqí 传奇. Except for a few nonfiction stories, this collection of some 500 short stories unfolds in a world that moves between the real and the surreal. In this world, vixen spirits, ghosts, and beasts interact with Chinese scholars, officials, Daoist exorcists, and businessmen. Interestingly enough, the author, Pú Sōnglíng 蒲松龄, seems to favor spirits and ghosts to human beings. He has made those ghost characters bold, loving, trustworthy, and physically more appealing than human beings.

Appearing as beautiful young girls, the fox-spirits in the book (known as húli jīng 狐狸精) are very different from the traditional women brought up under the influence of Confucianism. They are sexy but kind, loving but strong, naive but talented. The love stories between young men and these fox-spirits come about naturally rather than through the work of matchmakers, something quite common in a traditional society.

A page from "Strange Tales from Make-Do Studio," a collection of short stories published in the mid-Qing Dynasty

Pú Sōnglíng 蒲松龄 (1640 - 1715)

AKA: Pú Liǔquán 蒲柳泉, Liǔquán Jūshì 柳泉居士
From: Zībó 淄博, Shāndōng 山东
Known for: Author of *Strange Tales from Make-Do Studio*

Born in a merchant family, Pú Sōnglíng received his early education from his scholar-turned-merchant father. At 19, he passed the lowest level of the imperial examinations (xiùcái 秀才). After failing the imperial exams many times, he couldn't obtain any official posts. Thus, he spent most of his lifetime tutoring and writing, away from his own family and without much material comfort. It took him almost 40 years to write the 500 short stories in *Strange Tales from Make-Do Studio*. The fascinating stories were a big hit even in manuscript form. The stories are mainly about love relationships between men and supernatural beings, usually fox-women. Pú Sōnglíng didn't live long enough to enjoy the fame. The earliest print version we find today dates to 1766, supposedly published by his grandson.

Pu Songling's residence

The Fox Worship

The Chinese have very mixed feelings towards the fox. Commonly seen in northern China, this animal is generally believed to possess supernatural powers and to live forever. Temples and shrines were built in cities like Qīngdǎo 青岛 and Yāntái 烟台 for people to worship the Fox-Genius. Even today, there are still some old Chinese rural farmers who pay visits to village fox temples and pray for good fortune and long life.

Due to the fox's nocturnal habits, it's also believed that this small and crafty animal embodies the yīn 阴 or feminine characteristics. The yīn fox would come out whenever possible to look for the yáng 阳, the male element. Only by absorbing the yáng could the fox keep fit and live a long life. Thus, in the old days people used to believe that a fox-turned-woman would appear at night, trying to capture a man by seducing him with her charm. In the Chinese language, if a woman is described as a húli jīng 狐狸精 (fox-spirit), people know that the woman has the seductive prowess of a fox. To be seen as a húli jīng, however, often carries a somewhat negative connotation. It reflects the sexism deeply rooted in China's traditionally male-dominated society.

Fox temples were built for people to pray for good fortune and a long life.

Children's tiger-head caps are said to have the magic power of scaring off evil spirits. In today's rural China, they are still, together with tiger shoes and pillows, the most common gifts.

Into the Folk Arts

Visiting Shāndōng 山东 is like walking into a folk art museum. Kites, new year woodblock prints, paper cuts, clay figures and toys abound, inviting visitors of all ages to spend hours in stores and workshops. The local people are very skilled and take pleasure producing such a variety of folk arts. Most of these artists are ordinary farmers who labor during the day, then make crafts in the evening or during long winter days when they are resting and away from farm work.

An artist in Yangjiabu, Weifang, is making a woodblock print, using traditional techniques.

New Year Woodblock Prints

For many rural Chinese people today, celebrating Spring Festival is still closely associated with putting up new year woodblock prints or nián huà 年画, an old tradition dating back thousands of years. Welcoming the new year doesn't mean only celebrating its arrival, but also honoring one's ancestors and praying for good fortune. Thus common images in these prints include sages, heroes, harvest scenes, happy children, and frolicking animals surrounded by colorful flowers of auspicious significance.

Yángliǔqīng 杨柳青 in Tiānjīn 天津, Táohuāwù 桃花坞 in Sūzhōu 苏州, and Yángjiābǔ 杨家堡 in Wéifāng 潍坊 are famous for producing high quality new year woodblock prints for the past 500 years. As early as the Míng 明 Dynasty, a family by the surname of Yáng 杨 moved from Sìchuān 四川 Province and settled in a village later known as Yángjiābǔ. The Yáng family was trained in the technique of making woodblock prints and started to provide the market with its signature products. They spread the techniques to surrounding villages where woodblock printing workshops flourished.

Paper Cutting

The art of paper cutting is also closely related to holiday celebrations such as the Spring Festival, and special events such as weddings and home decorations. In the old days, paper was the cheapest material that most people could afford, so it was widely used. Young ladies who were not married were expected to acquire the skill of paper cutting, as it was considered part of a woman's set of skills known as nǚhóng 女红 which included needlework, embroidery, weaving, cutting and dyeing.

The carp is considered auspicious for the new year celebration.

Yangjiabu new year woodblock prints of guardian door gods

The subjects of paper cuts reflect folk customs and common desires for longevity, fertility and prosperity. For example, images of dragons and serpents in paper cuts symbolize the exorcism of evil spirits; peaches, deer, cranes and turtles are symbols of long life; lotuses, gourds, pomegranates and beautiful children represent the desire for more descendants.

As a folk art base, Shāndōng is famous for paper cutting. Places such as Gāomì 高密, Bīnzhōu 滨州, and several villages on the east coast are renowned for this art medium. You could never imagine that a female farmer you meet on the road can turn a piece of simple red paper into such a beautiful work of art.

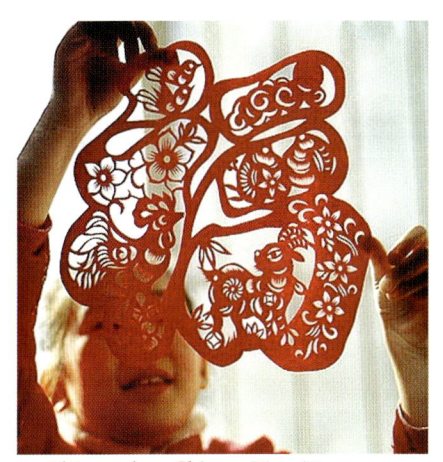

Artisans in Shandong make vivid clay figurines.

Clay Figurines and Toys

Clay figurines and toys are common folk art pieces found in Shāndōng. They are especially popular in the Wéifāng region because the soil there is fine and sticky. The molding of clay figurines dates back to the Warring States Period (475 - 221 B.C.E.). It is believed that Sūn Bìn 孙膑, the famous military strategist who lived between the fourth and third century B.C.E., first used clay figurines for mock military exercises. Clay figurines have been popular across the country since the Míng Dynasty. Clay figurines such as the Goddess of Mercy, the God of Longevity and other gods were made in large numbers and sold to visitors at Daoist and Buddhist temples. Later on, the art expanded to include toys, traditional figures, and plump babies.

Clay toys from Gaomi, Weifang, are loved and appreciated throughout China.

In China, when Chinese New Year comes, every household puts up the Chinese character "fu" meaning happiness.

The Love for Tigers

The tiger or hǔ 虎 is the third animal in the Chinese zodiac. For the Chinese, the tiger is the king of wild beasts, representing masculine traits such as bravery, competitiveness, and immense force. They are all good characteristics that Chinese want in a son. For thousands of years, newborn baby boys are presented with tiger-head caps and shoes, and tiger-shaped pillows. Many of them are even nicknamed hǔzī 虎子 or tiger cub. Parents of those boys love to hear that their sons "have a tiger's head and brains" or hǔtóu hǔnǎo 虎头虎脑.

Across China, the tiger is a popular theme in Chinese folk arts and traditional paintings. The animal is even a Daoist guardian god. There is a long-standing tradition that people buy two clay tigers and put them in the house on New Year's Eve (Spring Festival or chūnjié 春节), hoping to scare off evil spirits.

Tiger clay toys

Explore-A-Province in China®

Discovering Technology and Medicine

Have you ever connected ancient Chinese architecture and traditional Chinese medicine with the province of Shāndōng 山东? Actually, they both have roots there thanks to two great men: Lǔ Bān 鲁班 and Biǎn Què 扁鹊.

THE ART OF CARPENTRY

If you were told that the main hall in the Temple of Heaven in Běijīng 北京 was made without a single nail or glue, you would probably refuse to believe it. However, most ancient buildings were built in this way. The wood joint construction techniques are called mortise and tenon, and were said to have been discovered by a craftsman about 2,500 years ago.

This master artisan is Gōngshū Bān 公输班 (507 - 444 B.C.E.), also commonly known to the Chinese as Lǔ Bān. Born to skilled craftsmen in Qūfǔ 曲阜, Shāndōng, Lǔ Bān started working on construction sites very young and learned all the advanced skills of the time. Not satisfied with the tools he had, Lǔ Bān invented a set of carpentry tools, including the plain, axes, shovels, and ink markers.

One story has it that he invented the axe accidentally. Once he fell down from a mountain, and seriously cut his hand on a certain grass with sharp edges on both ends. This event gave him the idea for the axe. He experimented first with a piece of bamboo, and then a piece of iron. That's how he made the first axe.

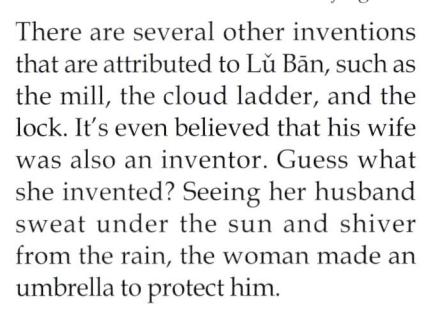

There are several other inventions that are attributed to Lǔ Bān, such as the mill, the cloud ladder, and the lock. It's even believed that his wife was also an inventor. Guess what she invented? Seeing her husband sweat under the sun and shiver from the rain, the woman made an umbrella to protect him.

Lǔ Bān's inventions led to revolutionary improvements in carpentry, masonry, bricklaying, and architecture. He is revered by skilled laborers and tradesmen, and still worshipped today. On May 7 of the lunar calendar, carpenters all kowtow and burn incense in front of Lǔ Bān's memorial tablet or páiwèi 牌位. On the second day of the Spring Festival, carpenters worship Lǔ Bān at home by putting one of his favorite tools on the altar and offering a sacrifice, with the hope of a prosperous and safe new year.

The construction of the China's National Science Museum in Beijing was inspired by the Lu Ban Lock.

Master Lu Ban is still worshipped in China today.

Ancient ink markers have now become collector's items.

Inside the main hall of Beijing's Temple of Heaven. The building is a magnificent showcase of the techniques of mortise and tenon joint-style construction.

Bian Que acupuncturing his patients as shown on a bas-relief from the Eastern Han Dynasty (25 - 220 C.E.)

Traditional Chinese Medicine - Diagnosis

Traditional Chinese Medicine (TCM) or zhōngyī 中医 has a philosophical approach different from that of Western medicine. Western doctors tend to treat the symptoms while TCM doctors regard the symptoms as manifesting a condition within the body. Biǎn Què 扁鹊, given name Qín Yuèrén 秦越人, developed diagnostic tools that today remain the foundation for TCM. His legendary success with the sick and the dying earned him the title of Biǎn Què, a medical deity.

Biǎn Què created a system of primary observation techniques with four parts. The first, observation or **wàng** 望, requires the physician to observe the patient's outward appearance for odd coloration or erratic behavior. The TCM principle that underlines this technique is that the patient's pallor is closely related to the state of his or her internal organs. The second observation technique, listening or **wén** 闻, requires the physician to listen carefully to sounds made by the patient and also to detect any odd smells emanating from the patient's body. In particular, TCM physicians listen to sounds the patient makes while speaking, breathing, and coughing.

Here the physician also needs to check for the presence, smells, and sounds of gases and other excretions. According to Biǎn Què and to TCM, bad or irregular smells often emerge when a patient's blood or internal organs are affected by illness. The third primary observation technique is called symptom assessment, or **wèn** 问, and is especially important when the first two techniques do not yield enough information. The physician looks for clues in the patient's family lineage and history of illness. Finally, the fourth and last technique,

Bian Que taking the pulse. A clay sculpture made by Chinese artist Yang Zhizhong in 1978

pulse recognition or **qiè** 切, requires the physician to determine whether or not the patient's body is functioning normally.

His primary observation techniques can be summed up as: a) Wàng 望 (observing the patient for color and erratic behavior; b) Wén 闻 (listening to the voice); c) Wèn 问 (symptom assessment); d) Qiè 切 (taking the pulse).

Biǎn Què toured the many kingdoms, broadening his learning wherever his constituents required. He was a pediatrician to children, a gynecologist to women, and a geriatric physician to the old and infirmed. His treatments included acupuncture, procuring of medicines, and surgery. Despite his national popularity, he was assassinated by a Qín 秦 Dynasty royal medical officer, Lǐ Xī 李醯, because Lǐ Xī could not contain his jealousy.

Biǎn Què has been memorialized all over China. He had nine disciples who worked closely with him and assured that his nine-volume classic entitled *Internal Canon of Medicine*, 12 volumes of *External Canon of Medicine* and 13 volumes of *Biǎn Què' Prescriptions Approved by First Yellow Emperor* were passed down. His basic theories continue to guide TCM in the modern world.

Biǎn Què 扁鹊 (circa 407 - 310 B.C.E.)

AKA: Qín Yuèrén 秦越人
From: Chángqīng 长清, Shāndōng 山东 Province
Known For: His diagnostic doctrine for assessing illness and discomfort

Biǎn Què was probably the first and most popular doctor of general medicine, traveling through China to help the ill, the needy, and the impoverished. Legend says he could bring the dying back to life. Thus, he was nicknamed Biǎn Què, the medical deity. He left behind a great deal of catalogued information still fundamental reference material for TCM practitioners today.

*Without Zhongni (Confucius),
the history would have been endless night.*
Zhu Xi, late 12th century Confucian philosopher

The Story of Confucius

孔子的故事

Mr. Zhu Zhizhong and his students in a private family Confucian school in Yueyang, Hunan Province. Mr. Zhu was 80 years old when the photo was taken December 6, 2004. The school, a rarity in today's China, was about to close due to his age.

20 Common Sayings in "The Analects"

Is it not a pleasure to learn and practice what is learned? Is it not a delight to have friends come from distant places? (Book 1 - Chapter 1)

Xué ér shí xí zhī, bú yì yuè hū? Yǒu péng zì yuǎnfāng lái, bú yì lè hū?

学而时习之，不亦说乎?
有朋自远方来，不亦乐乎?

Be true to one's word. (1-7)

Yán ér yǒu xìn.

言而有信。

At 30, I stood firm; At 40, I had no doubts; At 50, I knew the decrees of Heaven; At 60, my ear was attuned to the truth; At 70, I could follow what my heart desired, without breaking from what was right. (2-4)

Sānshí ér lì, sìshí ér búhuò, wǔshí ér zhī tiānmìng, liùshí ér ěr shùn, qīshí ér cóng xīn suǒ yù, bù yú jù.

三十而立，四十而不惑，五十而知天命，六十而耳顺，七十而从心所欲，不逾矩。

Learning without thought is labor lost; thought without learning is perilous. (2-15)

Xué ér bù sī zé wǎng, sī ér bù xué zé dài.

学而不思则罔，思而不学则殆。

Rotten wood cannot be carved. (5-10)

Xiǔmù bùkě diāo yě.

朽木不可雕也。

Be not ashamed to ask and learn from one's inferiors. (5-15)

Bùchǐ xià wèn.

不耻下问。

Look before you leap. (5-20)

Sānsī ér hòu xíng.

三思而后行。

A youth is to be regarded with respect. (9-26)

Hòushēng kěwèi.

后生可畏。

Even the will of a common man cannot be taken from him. (9-29)

Pǐfū bùkě duó zhì.

匹夫不可夺志。

Do not impose upon others what you do not desire yourself. (12-3)

Jǐ suǒ bú yù, wù shī yú rén.

己所不欲，勿施于人。

All men are brothers within the four seas. (12-12)

Sìhǎi zhī nèi jiē xiōngdì.

四海之内皆兄弟。

A desire to have things done quickly prevents their being done thoroughly. Looking at small advantages prevents great affairs from being accomplished. (13-17)

Yù sù zé bù dá, jiàn xiǎolì zé dàshì bùchéng.

欲速则不达，见小利则大事不成。

Repay injury with justice, and repay kindness with kindness. (14-34)

Yǐ zhí bào yuàn, yǐ dé bào dé.

以直报怨，以德报德。

Let one's words be sincere and truthful and his actions honorable and careful. (15-6)

Yán dǔxìn, xíng dǔ jìng.

言笃信，形笃敬。

If a man doesn't think about what is distant, he will find sorrow near at hand. (15-12)

Rén wú yuǎnlǜ, bìyǒu jìnyōu.

人无远虑，必有近忧。

No bearing in small matters confounds great plans. (15-27)

Xiǎo bùrěn zé luàn dàmóu.

小不忍则乱大谋。

In teaching there should be no distinction of classes. (15-39)

Yǒu jiào wú lèi.

有教无类。

Those whose courses are different cannot lay plans for one another. (15-40)

Dào bùtóng, bù xiāng wéi móu.

道不同，不相为谋。

By nature, men are nearly alike; by practice, they get to be wide apart. (17-2)

Xìng xiāngjìn, xí xiāngyuǎn.

性相近，习相远。

A gentleman is generous but not wasteful; he is diligent but without complaint; he has desires but is not greedy; he is great but not arrogant; and he is strong but not fierce. (20-6)

Jūnzǐ huì ér bú fèi; láo ér búyuàn; yù ér bù tān; tài ér bù jiāo; wēi ér bù měng.

君子惠而不费；劳而不怨；欲而不贪；泰而不骄；威而不猛。

"The Analects of Confucius," a collection of dialogues between Confucius and his student-disciples, has been studied in China for 2,500 years.

The most common portrait of Confucius

The Life of Confucius

Confucius or Kǒng Zǐ 孔子 was fated from the outset to a life of unending hardship. He was born in 551 B.C.E. during the Spring and Autumn Period (770 - 476 B.C.E.), a product of the marriage between his then 60-year-old father and his 20-year-old wife. He lived in a typical rural village at the foot of Níqiūshān 尼丘山 called Lǔyuán 鲁源. Confucius' father, although a man of military merit, was a civil servant at the low end of a strictly-respected hierarchy of official postings. Confucius was three years old when his father passed away, whereupon the young mother Yán Zhēngzài 颜征在 and her infant son took up residence in Quèlǐ 阙里, on the outskirts of Qūfǔ 曲阜, the capital of the State of Lǔ 鲁.

At that time, some 2,500 years ago, Quèlǐ was a working class town, a good distance away from Qūfǔ and its inner city, home to the aristocracy. It is said that Confucius exhibited an unusual sensitivity to social standing, and the rampant class-consciousness ever prevalent in Chinese society. Advancement required study and mastery of a number of skills, primarily those known as the "six arts" — rites (lǐ 礼), music (yuè 乐), archery (shè 射), charioting (yù 御), calligraphy (shū 书), and mathematics (shù 术). Confucius went on to master these skills, but he showed an early passion for the ancient rites and rituals practiced during the early Western Zhōu 周 Dynasty (1046 - 771 B.C.E.).

Confucius first taught at a place called Xingtan (The Apricot Altar). Later, an altar was built there in his honor.

Part of "Deeds of Confucius" of the Ming Dynasty (1368 - 1644). Confucius engaged in teaching throughout his lifetime. It was said that he had 3,000 regular students.

The State of Lǔ was a small state under the auspices of the Western Zhōu Dynasty, famous for its practice of rituals. This undoubtedly had a profound influence on the young Confucius who viewed war and the use of force as big threats to state stability and benevolent living.

Confucius' mother passed away in 535 B.C.E., whereupon the dutiful son went into a state of mourning for three years. It was an exceptional action for a young man of 17. Some two years later, Confucius married and soon after had a son.

Then he entered public service first as a granary observer and later as a minister in the State of Lǔ. Unfortunately, the kingdom was constantly at war and in moral and spiritual decline. Confucius' reflections on the time developed in thought vis-à-vis benevolence, propriety, ritual, and moral living.

In 522 B.C.E, when Confucius saw little hope of himself holding a higher post in the government, he started a school at a place called Xìngtán 杏坛 in Qūfǔ. This was the first school outside the government system that gave both the rich and the poor equal opportunities for education. At his school, free discussion among students and teachers was encouraged. Dialogues between Confucius and his student-disciples were recorded and later compiled, by his students, into *The Analects of Confucius* or Lúnyǔ 论语, the most important source of Confucius' ideas.

At the age of 54, Confucius left the land of Lǔ and began his 14-year journey from state to state, traveling by horse-drawn cart and followed by a growing number of disciples. As he traveled, his ideas spread throughout the vastness of the nation, including the states of Wèi 卫, Chén 陈, Zhèng 郑, Sòng 宋, Cài 蔡, and Chǔ 楚. Confucius and his growing band of followers met with continual hardship and opposition including banditry, tyranny, widespread poverty, and ignorance of the agrarian classes. As he continued to wander, he drew as many as 3,000 students, who later went on to spread their master's ideas in nearly every state in the land.

At 68 years old, Confucius retired from his travels; 14 years on the road brought him fame, notoriety, respect and contempt – but not one official appointment through which he might have been able to implement his policies. Ironically, when Confucius passed away in 479 B.C.E, the master had no idea of the mark he would leave on future generations: his policies penetrated Chinese culture and institutions, and his memory was deified.

Did you know?

- Confucius is a latinized version of "Kǒng Fūzǐ 孔夫子," meaning "Master of Kǒng 孔." After Kǒng Zǐ's 孔子 death, he was commonly referred to as Kǒng Fūzǐ.

- Confucius was not only a philosopher, thinker, and educator but also a musician, connoisseur, Go player, and archer.

- Confucius edited, in his late years, *The Book of Songs* or Shī 诗, *The Book of History* or Shū 书, *The Book of Rites* or Lǐ 礼, *The Book of Music* or Yuè 乐, and *The Spring and Autumn Annals* or Chūnqiū 春秋, making great contributions in preserving ancient cultural heritage. These five books are known as the "Five Classics" or Wǔjīng 五经 and are extremely important readings for Confucian learning and understanding.

- Spanning 2,500 years, the family tree of Confucius has extended to 83 generations with over two million descendants.

Bronze statue of "Confucius wandering in various states in China," Qufu, Shandong

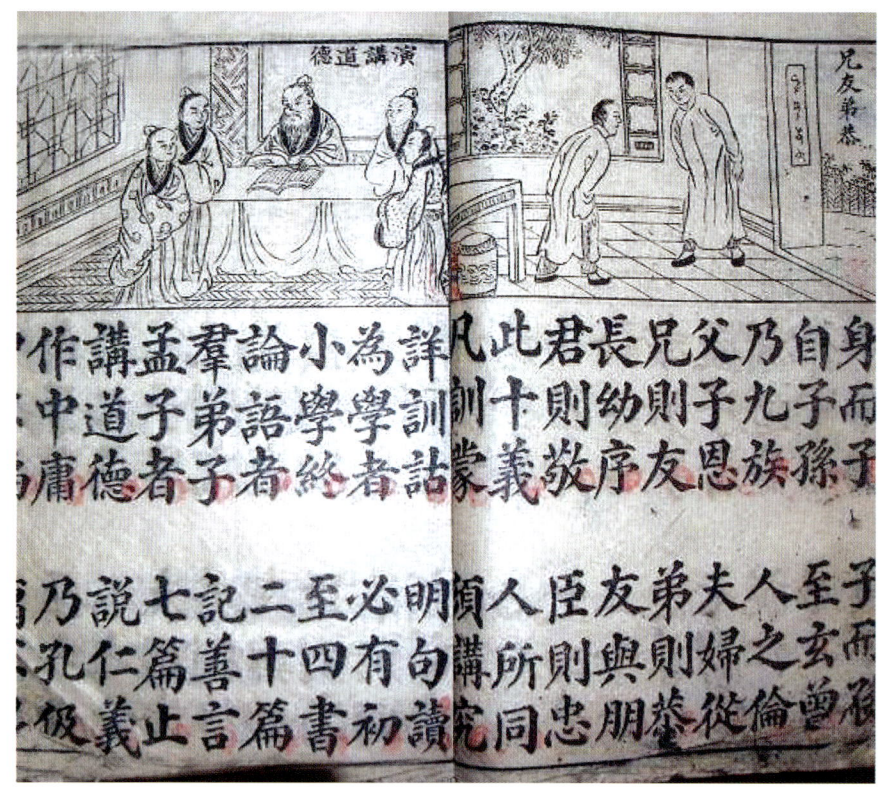

Sanzijing, the "Three Character Classic" written during the 13th century, was the most widely studied textbook for Chinese students. It is primarily a condensed and simplified book of Confucian essential teachings that help young children learn to read and write.

Portrait of Three Saints from left to right: Zeng Can, Confucius, and Yan Hui. Zeng Can and Yan Hui were two of Confucius' 72 close disciples.

Confucian Ideas

Confucian ideas are mainly known from *The Analects of Confucius* or lúnyǔ 论语, a collection of dialogues between Confucius and his student-disciples.

The following is an annotated version of the doctrine of Confucius, providing an introduction and, hopefully, an inspiration to continue your studies of the great teacher in more detail. An abundance of English language discourse on his ancient musings is available.

士 Shì or Gentleman

A term applied to the lower classes of the nobility, warriors and officials. His prominent use of such titles defined the moral standard of the individual.

礼 Lǐ or Ritual

"Lǐ," was a term used to describe the manners, customs, rituals and elaborate protocols of the nobility. The demands of lǐ implied more than just a rote repetition of ceremony and ritual, but implied a commitment to reverence during such practices. Thus lǐ also carries the meaning of "proper conduct."

道 Dào or the Way

Dào has long been translated by Daoists as "The Way." Confucius' version of the explanation was the "moral way," implying that everyone in society should live a virtuous life by showing respect to station and working within the hierarchy.

Main Moral Concepts

Benevolence or human kindness was a foundation of Confucius' teaching, and in Chinese this quality is known as "rén 仁."

Lǐ is the adherence to proper rites and rituals, further providing guidelines for proper conduct. The adherence to the ancient rites was another way of reinforcing a code of formal behavior in an ever-changing world. They provided stability, consistency and most importantly, the sanctity of tradition.

"Dé 德," also known as virtue, was the third aspiration of an individual, following his rén and lǐ. This culmination represented the pinnacle of Confucian development since virtue expressed itself through action. Mere contemplation was insufficient to deliver the individual to his or her fullest potential. Thus one's final goal was to endow virtue with actionable qualities, making these three moral concepts not mere philosophy, but a formal guide to living.

Morality and Relationships

To establish a harmonious society, Confucius believed in the "Five Cardinal Relationships" and further held that each member of society, from an emperor down to a peasant, was expected to perform his or her functions according to hierarchy and he or she must respect those above in a hierarchical system.

These five relationships were subject to emperor, son to father, wife to husband, younger brother to elder brother, and finally younger friend to elder friend.

Actually, all relations were based on social and familial hierarchies. Confucius expected that should each member of society carry out his or her obligations of lǐ, rén and dé then harmony would result between people and within families; there would also be fairness in matters of public service. Ultimately, adherence to these moral concepts was a way of appeasing the mandate or will of heaven, thereby assuring a long and prosperous life of the individual and

Confucius is considered the greatest teacher in history. Many Chinese students still honor him when they pass important examinations.

Mèng Zǐ 孟子 (372 - 289 B.C.E.)

AKA: Mencius, Mèng Kē 孟轲, Yàshèng 亚圣
From: Zōuchéng 邹城 City, Shāndōng 山东
Known For: The greatest Confucian thinker after Confucius

Mèng Zǐ or Mencius sought to defend the teachings of Confucius against other influential movements of thought, especially those associated with Mò Zǐ 墨子 (470 - 382 B.C.E.) and Yáng Zhū 杨朱 (370 - 319 B.C.E.). He is probably best known for the view that "human nature is good." This view of human nature defended the Confucian ideal and developed the self-cultivation process. His view was subsequently challenged by Xún Zǐ 荀子, another major Confucian thinker, who defended the alternative view that "human nature is evil."

Confucian thinkers of the Hàn 汉 Dynasty (206 B.C.E - 220 C.E.) were influenced by the teachings of both, but by the late Táng 唐 (618 - 907 C.E.) Dynasty, influential intellectuals such as Hán Yù 韩愈 (768 - 824 C.E.) came to regard Mèng Zǐ as the true transmitter of Confucius' teachings. This view was shared by Confucian thinkers of the early Sòng 宋 Dynasty (960 - 1279 C.E). Zhū Xī 朱熹 (1130 - 1200 C.E.) included *The Mencius* as one of the Four Books, which became canonical texts of the Confucian tradition. Mèng Zǐ came to be regarded as the greatest Confucian thinker after Confucius himself, and his teachings have been very influential on the development of Confucian thought in the Sòng, Míng 明 (1368 - 1644), and Qīng 清 (1616 - 1911) dynasties, and up to modern times.

Xún Zǐ 荀子 (circa 313 - 238 B.C.E.)

AKA: Xún Kuàng 荀况, Xún Qīng 荀卿
Born: Ānzé 安泽, Héběi 河北 Province (He spent most of his lifetime in Shāndōng.)
Known For: Revision of Confucianism

Xún Zǐ further revised Confucianism, breaking from both the original texts and the later works of Mèng Zǐ. Active during the Warring States Period, Xún Zǐ saw people as having an inherently evil nature that required control by education, ritual and custom. His student, Hán Fēi Zǐ 韩非子, developed this philosophy further by elevating law to a position of supreme importance in governing human affairs. Hán Fēi Zǐ's alleged influence on the Emperor Qīn 秦 (in such activities as cruel punishments and the attempt to destroy China's past by burning books) gave him notoriety that reflected back poorly on his teacher. As a result, the work of Mèng Zǐ for many centuries received much more attention than that of Xún Zǐ.

Xún Zǐ became a well-recognized scholar and rose to official posts, including that of magistrate. In spite of his gloomy view of humanity's original nature, Xún Zǐ saw people as perfectible through education and application of the proper rules of conduct. People were born with a conflicting mixture of desires, that, if allowed unfettered reign, would lead to disaster. It was the role of society, through its culture (including music) to impose order onto the chaos of desires and channel them into constructive, rather than destructive, effort. He held that human intelligence created social organizations in order to bring divergent human impulses into harmony. To this end, Xún Zǐ stressed not only the importance of education but also the correct use of words, often providing extensive lists of definitions. He is also noteworthy in his view that heaven is not the realm of mystical forces embodying ethical principles (Mèng Zǐ's view), but that it is part of the realm of nature, indifferent to humans.

Confucianism after the Master

Confucius lives on in his teachings and the philosophical school known as Confucianism or rújiā 儒家. Attributed to the Master, this system is rooted in his beliefs and developed over time.

During Confucius' lifetime, not a single state had appointed him to high office, nor adopted his ideals or policies. But his teachings continued to spread and were studied among Chinese scholars including Mèng Zǐ 孟子 and Xún Zǐ 荀子, who are considered two influential Confucian thinkers. Confucian teachings were severely attacked by the first Chinese Emperor, Qín Shǐ Huáng 秦始皇 of the Qín 秦 Dynasty (221 - 206 B.C.E.). He carried out a move called "Burning Books and Burying Scholars" or fénshū kēngrú 焚书坑儒. The emperor buried some 400 loyal followers of Confucius alive and burnt most of the books compiled by Confucius and his followers. After Qín Shǐ Huáng perished, surviving Confucians rewrote the classics. Nine years after the fall of the Qín, the Hàn 汉 Dynasty (206 B.C.E. - 220 C.E.) established itself as a unified central state, its leaders committed to establishing a stable social order.

When the Hàn 汉 Emperor Wǔ Dì 武帝 was in power, he took the advice of one of his ministers, Dǒng Zhòngshū 董仲舒 (179 - 104 B.C.E.), to implement Confucianism as the state ideology. Centuries after the death of the great teacher, his ideas were finally institutionalized, marginalizing or abolishing all other schools of thought. Starting with the Hàn Emperor Wǔ Dì, nearly all emperors afterwards held Confucianism as the orthodox thinking.

Successive dynasties continued the tradition of Confucian rule by virtue, until the late 12th century, when Zhū Xī 朱熹 (1130 - 1200 C.E.), a Confucian master and senior official of the Sòng 宋 Dynasty (960 - 1279 C.E.) set about a dogmatic and restrictive revision of Confucian teaching, one that has left its mark on present-day China. Zhū Xī and other Confucian thinkers were collectively referred to as Neo-Confucianists. They argued that only by studying the Confucian Classics could a person learn correct behavior or lǐ 礼. The Sòng emperors believed in Zhū Xī's Neo-Confucianism and ordered that the imperial examinations solely test on students' understanding of Confucian teachings.

Confucianism, however, was criticized in China during the May Fourth and the New Culture movements at the beginning of the 20th century. An opponent of Confucianism, Máo Zédōng 毛泽东 wiped the teaching of Confucianism from all Chinese schools after 1949. Revisions have been made in China's mainland since Chairman Máo's death. Today, Confucian influence reaches far beyond China into other Asian nations like Japan, Korea, Malaysia, and Singapore.

Mao Zedong made Confucius a target of criticism during the 10-year Cultural Revolution (1966 - 1976), casting him as a representative of old values.

Portrait of Confucius by famous artist Ma Yuan of the Yuan Dynasty (1368 - 1644)

Zhu Xi (1130 -1200 C.E.) was one of the most important Confucian thinkers. He created a dogmatic and restrictive revision of Confucian teaching.

Statue of Confucius in the Temple of Confucius, Qufu, Shandong. Confucius was deified to a god-like figure in Chinese culture for centuries.

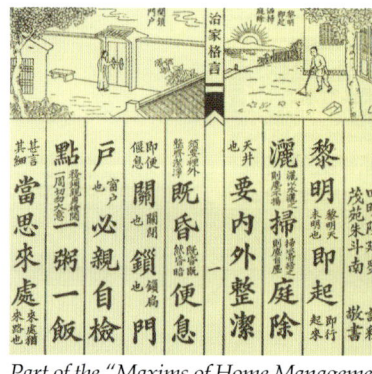

Part of the "Maxims of Home Management," also known as Zhu Zi Geyan. It was a book of 500 words written in the 17th century by a man named Zhu Bolu. The book was used by every Chinese family to regulate the behavior of sons and daughters in the traditional (Confucian) way.

Confucian Influences

Filial piety

Filial piety or xiàodào 孝道 is one of the most important elements of Confucian moral values. It refers to dedication, respect, and obedience to one's parents. In a Chinese society, a person is likely to be judged by how he or she treats his or her parents (and in-laws). Moreso, according to tradition, everyone should respect those people who are over 60 years old.

ANCESTRAL WORSHIP

"If you want to rule a state, first put your house (family) in order." This Confucian principle established the family unit as the basis for the Five Cardinal Relationships. Chinese pay particular attention to the clan, the big family of descendants from one remote common ancestor. Today, even though the tradition of ancestral worship is gradually dying, you can still come across numerous ancestral halls or cítáng 祠堂. There, clan records or jiāpǔ 家谱, and ancestral tablets (ancestors' names engraved into wooden boards) or páiwèi 牌位 are carefully preserved.

Confucius Institutes

Confucius Institutes are non-profit schools that promote Chinese language learning and cultural exchange all over the world. The project is supervised by the Office of Chinese Language Council International, commonly known as Hanban, in conjunction with its partner organization (university or Chinese culture association) abroad. As of November 2008, there were 307 Confucius Institutes in 78 countries and regions. As the supervisor of the most successfully government-run cultural project, the Beijing-based Hanban hopes to open 1,000 Confucius Institutes by 2020. Outside of Hanban, there are institutions all over the world promoting Chinese language learning. It is estimated that by 2020 there will be approximately 100 million non-Chinese people worldwide learning Chinese as a non-native language.

Teachers' Day

A great educator, Confucius has long been considered "the teacher of all teachers." To honor him and all Chinese teachers, his birthday, September 28, has been celebrated as Teachers' Day or jiàoshī jié 教师节 since the 1930s. The celebration was stopped on China's mainland from 1951 until 1984. Today, on Teachers' Day, which has been moved to September 10, students honor their teachers by presenting cards, flowers, and craft work.

Table manners

Table manners often follow Confucian ideals. The most highly respected guest, often the eldest, sits on the north side of the table or directly facing the door. Other guests can only eat after this person picks up his chopsticks. Even today, in most Chinese rural areas, women are not allowed to sit at the same table as men for big occasions.

The Four Arts of a Scholar

Confucianists hold that a scholar needs to cultivate his tastes in areas like the qín 琴, a zither-like seven-stringed instrument (music), qí 棋 (chess), shū 书 (calligraphy) and huà 画 (painting). This belief collectively termed as the "Fours Arts of a Scholar" has been a very influential force in parenting. (Photo taken of a girl taking a violin lesson in a private school called Mèngmǔtáng 孟母堂 in Shànghǎi 上海.)

A bird's-eye view of the Temple of Confucius in Qufu

A Walk through Qufu

(An excerpt from Emma's Diary, dated August 25)

To be honest, apart from Tàishān 泰山, Qūfǔ 曲阜 was my motivation for coming to Shāndōng 山东. I have been curious about Confucius for quite some time, and making a trip to his hometown definitely serves my purpose.

As Qūfǔ is only some 130 km south of Jǐnán 济南, my tour guide, Xiǎo Mèng 小孟, and I arrived there quite early in the morning. The "Three Kongs" – Kǒngmiào 孔庙 or the Temple of Confucius, Kǒngfǔ 孔府 or the Kong Family Mansion, and Kǒnglín 孔林 or the Cemetery of Confucius – did not open until 8:00 am. So we sat at an outdoor food tavern on Quèlǐ 阙里 Road, bought some fried dough (yóutiáo 油条) and soy milk (dòujiāng 豆浆), and began enjoying our morning in this very special city.

Of the 650,000 residents, more than 125,000 have the surname Kǒng 孔. This means that almost a quarter of the population is a descendant of the Master. I would guess that these people share the same forefather, the same history, and perhaps a similar look. When I said this to Xiǎo Mèng, he laughed at my naiveness. "These people actually don't share the same family history," Xiǎo Mèng said. "They are differentiated by whether they are direct descendants or whether they descend from a first son or first grandson of Confucius."

As I stood in the huge compound of the Kong Family Mansion (which has 463 halls!), I was quite amazed at the lavishness of this most important private estate. The compound was restored and rebuilt many times, and it was expanded to today's scale during the late Míng 明 Dynasty (1368 - 1644). There used to be about 500

The Dacheng Hall is supported by 28 white marble columns with magnificently-carved dragons.

Music and dance performances are put on in honor of Confucius between September and October of each year.

Inside the main hall of the Kong Family Mansion

The Dacheng Hall in the Temple of Confucius

servants serving the one family. The emperor gave this family's patriarch the title Duke of Yǎnshèng 衍圣, because he was the first descendant of Confucius. For many generations, this branch of the Kǒng family enjoyed the luxury, power and privileges next to those only of a Chinese emperor. But what happened to those who were not born to the family of the first son? Xiǎo Mèng told me that their lives didn't even compare to the lives of Yǎnshèng family. In fact, many of them lived simple, modest lives.

Walking out of the Kong Family Mansion, which now serves as a family museum with relics and artifacts, we entered the Temple of Confucius, a 50-acre complex. The construction of this complex began one year after Confucius passed away in 479 B.C.E., right on the site of the three-room house where he used to live. The magnificent complex was a product of several reconstructions, mostly done in the Qīng 清 Dynasty (1616 - 1911). It took us a long time to tour all nine courtyards that run south to north. The huge place is also scattered with ancient gnarled trees and some 2,000 stone-carved tablets by a number of Chinese emperors, literary elites, calligraphers, and famous historical figures.

Sitting at the Temple of Confucius is the Dàchéng 大成 Hall, supported by 28 white marble columns with magnificently carved dragons. Xiǎo Mèng told me that whenever Qīng emperors came to pay homage to Confucius, these dragons were covered up, because they were more beautiful and magnificent than those in Běijīng's 北京 Forbidden City. Dragons in this country are imperial symbols and a supreme representation of the yáng 阳 element, so all imperial buildings have dragon images.

Inside the Dàchéng Hall are the statues of Confucius and 12 of his chief followers. Among them, I recognized Zhū Xī 朱熹, the Confucian philosopher from Ānhuī 安徽 Province. Xiǎo Mèng told me that out on the terrace of the Dàchéng Hall, music and dance performances and ceremonial rites are put on during the Qūfǔ International Cultural Festival held from September 26 to October 10 of each year.

By noon, we were on Quèlǐ Road again, pleasantly tired after our long walk through the Confucian halls. We decided to hire a horse carriage for the two-mile ride to the next destination: the Cemetery of Confucius. On our way there, I noticed that most of the cypress trees lining both sides of the "Divine Road" don't have a main tree fork. Xiǎo Mèng explained that during the reign of Qīng Dynasty Emperor Qiánlóng 乾隆, the forks were chopped down by families who were not direct descendants of Confucius so as to express their envy of the direct descendants. After hearing the story, I was speechless and sad. What if I had been born into one of those families of Kǒngs who were only distantly related to Confucius? What if I had been a woman in one of those families?

The visit to the Cemetery of Confucius was not encouraging. Though there were about 100,000 Confucian members buried in the 500-acre cemetery, there were strict rules about who could be buried there. Those who were not allowed include monks, people who broke the law, daughters who had gotten married, and children who had died young. Here, once again, the Confucian concept of family hierarchy and its view of women struck me as incomprehensible. For the rest of the afternoon and evening, my mind was with those less favored in a Confucian-based society.

The master's tomb at the Cemetery of Confucius

Provincial Highlights

Scenic Spots

There is a popular saying in China about Shāndōng 山东. It's said that the province beats other provinces by just three things: one mountain (Mt. Tài 泰), one river (Yellow River) and one sage (Confucius). There is definitely some truth to this statement. The treasures of Shāndōng, both scenic and historic, are very symbolic of the Chinese nation.

Laoshan

Láoshān 崂山 (Láo Mountain) in Qīngdǎo 青岛 stands out as one of the best mountains in China because of its imposing canyon, undulating peaks, mysterious mist, and crystal-clear springs. In ancient times, it was widely believed that Láoshān was home to certain supernatural spirits (immortals) or xiānrén 仙人. Two ancient Chinese emperors, Qín Shǐ Huáng 秦始皇 of the Qín 秦 Dynasty (221 - 206 B.C.E.) and Wǔ Dì 武帝 of the Hàn 汉 Dynasty (206 B.C.E. - 220 C.E.) both visited Láoshān hoping to meet immortals and learn the secret to eternal life.

A Daoist mountain, Láoshān has nine palaces, eight temples and 72 nunneries that used to house over 1,000 priests and nuns. Legend has it that the Daoist priests had acquired magical powers to make themselves invisible and walk through walls. Famous figures in Daoism like Qiū Chángchūn 邱长春 (an advisor to Genghis Khan) and Zhāng Sānfēng 张三丰 (the one who is said to have developed a school of martial arts called Wǔdāng 武当 Boxing) lived on Láoshān during the Yuán 元 Dynasty (1206 - 1368).

Weishan Lake

Covering an area of 1,200 sq km, Wēishān 微山 Lake is one of the largest freshwater lakes in China, comprised of Wēishān 微山, Zhāoyáng 昭阳, Dúshān 独山 and Nányáng 南阳 lakes. In summer, lotus flowers blossom and create a splendid view. Watching the locals catch fish is a leisurely way to spend one's day. Find some time to dine with the local fishermen. Their wives make delicious dishes using arrowroot and carp. Wēishān lake is considered to be one of southern Shāndōng's treasures.

Spend a day at Weishan Lake to enjoy home-style dishes made by fishermen's wives!

Weishan Lake is one of southern Shandong's treasures.

Laoshan is a must-see site in Qingdao.

Mengshan

Most Chinese people know Méngshān 蒙山 (Mt. Méng) from a song in a revolutionary film called *The Red Sun*: "Green mountains adjoin, white clouds fly." (Yī zuò zuò qīngshān jǐn xiāng lián, yī duǒ duǒ báiyún rào shān jiān 一座座青山紧相连，一朵朵白云绕山间。) Now Méngshān has turned into a national forest park. With 72 peaks, 99 valleys and 36 caverns in the area, Méngshān is historically known as "a mountain resort for longevity." Many famous historical figures such as Wáng Xīzhī 王羲之, a great calligrapher of the Jìn 晋 Dynasty (265 - 420 C.E.), and Zhūgě Liàng 诸葛亮, a revered wise man of the Three Kingdoms Period (220 - 280 C.E.), were born in the Méngshān area.

Swan Lake

During November and April, large numbers of swans and other birds fly south to one lake in Dōngyíng 东营 City to spend the winter. The lake is called Swan Lake or Tiān'é Hú 天鹅湖 and is the largest man-made lake on the North China Plain. The lake couldn't be better situated, as it lies near Dōngyíng where the Yellow River flows into the Bóhǎi 渤海 Sea. Provided with a magnificent location and relatively warm weather in the winter, Dōngyíng attracts both swans and visitors.

The Yellow River Estuary

Not far from Swan Lake, also in Dōngyíng City, is the vast wetland known as the Yellow River Estuary, which covers an area of 153,000 sq hectares. There are 1,524 kinds of animals and 268 kinds of birds living in the area, thus the place has been a big draw for birdwatchers. In the spring, reeds sway in the wind, their white flowers flying like the snow. Visiting the Yellow River Estuary is an unforgettable experience.

Mainly in southwestern Shandong, Mengshan (Mt. Meng) is historically known as a "mountain resort for longevity." Today it has turned into a national forest park.

Dongying City's Swan Lake is home to flocks of swans and other birds every winter.

The Yellow River Estuary, a birdwatcher's heaven, is growing into a wetland of national importance.

Explore-A-Province in China®

泰山
Taishan

According to Chinese myths and legends, Tàishān 泰山 or Mt. Tài in Shāndōng 山东 Province was formed with the head of Pán Gǔ 盘古, who the Chinese believe created the earth. When Pán Gǔ finished making the earth, he was exhausted. As he lay down to die, his head was transformed into Tàishān, and his arms and legs became the other four sacred mountains, namely Mt. Huà or Huàshān 华山 in Shaanxi Province, Mt. Héng or Héngshān 衡山 in Húnán 湖南 Province, another Mt. Héng or Héngshān 恒山 in Shānxī 山西 Province, and Mt. Sōng or Sōngshān 嵩山 in Hénán 河南 Province.

Historically, Tàishān was the place where Chinese emperors offered sacrifices to heaven and earth. Rulers made trips to Tàishān as a public sign that they had inherited the world and would act upon calls from heaven. Beginning with the first Chinese emperor, Qín Shǐ Huáng 秦始皇 of the Qín 秦 Dynasty (221 - 206 B.C.E.), 13 Chinese emperors made pilgrimages to the mountain, thus bestowing upon Tàishān the most imperial significance of all the mountains in China. It was from this mountain that Confucius or Kǒng Zǐ 孔子 proclaimed the world to be small, and that Chairman Máo or Máo Zédōng 毛泽东 (1893 - 1976) pronounced the country Red (communist). No other Chinese mountain has such political significance.

Tàishān is located in the center of Shāndōng Province, not far from Jǐnán 济南, the provincial capital, and Qūfū 曲阜, the birthplace of Confucius. Though not very high (the highest peak, Jade Emperor Peak, is 1,545 metres above sea level), the mountain abounds in cultural remnants of the past. There are 22 temples, 97 ruins, 819 stone tablets, and 1,018 cliff-side stone inscriptions. Tàishān is also an important center for the religious practices of all China's major religions, namely Daoism, Buddhism, and Confucianism. Visitors from different parts of the country come to this mountain to pray in various temples for good fortune.

Aside from the historical splendor, many people climb Tàishān for the natural beauty: its lofty peaks, deep valleys, spectacular waterfalls, magnificent rocks, and its centuries-old pines and cypresses. The climb takes four to five hours. From the top, you can witness the four wonders of the mountain: sunrise, sunset, the sea of clouds and the golden belt of the Yellow River or Huánghé 黄河. Because of its natural beauty, and historical and cultural importance, Tàishān has been a UNESCO World Natural and Cultural Heritage Site since 1987.

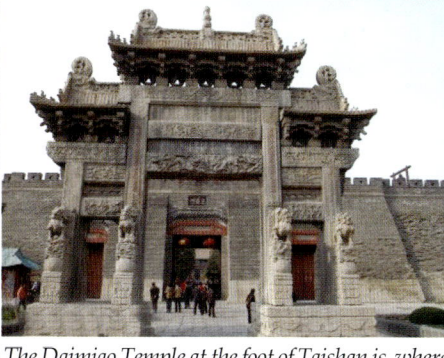

The Daimiao Temple at the foot of Taishan is where Chinese emperors offered sacrifices to Heaven and Earth. Daimiao's vast temple complex reflects the magnitude of ancient Chinese architecture.

For those climbing Taishan, the last part of the hike - the steep Path of Eighteen Bends - can be painful.

Most of the stone inscriptions on the cliffs are quotations from luminaries throughout Chinese history.

Climbers from different regions come to Taishan to pray for good fortune.

Historic Places

Penglai Pavilion

A coastal city under Yāntái's 烟台 administration, Pénglái 蓬莱 is well-known as the "the Fairyland on Earth." When the first Chinese Emperor Qín Shǐ Huáng 秦始皇 of the Qín 秦 Dynasty visited Pénglái, he was in desperate pursuit of elixirs (medicine alleged to extend life), as well as Daoist supernatural spirits, namely the Eight Immortals or bāxiān 八仙. Legend has it that these eight figures crossed the sea from Pénglái to live in eternity.

Built in 1061 C.E. of the Sòng 宋 Dynasty (960 - 1279 C.E.), the Pénglái Pavilion is situated on majestic cliffs facing the sea. For centuries, scholars, poets and artists have set foot upon this pavilion (one of the four major towers in China), leaving behind numerous writings, poems, calli-graphies and paintings about this miraculous land. Pénglái is often referred to as a mirage, an illusionary land not of this earth.

The most magnificent ancient fortification with built-in cannons in Penglai was built to ward off Janpanese pirates during the Ming Dynasty (1368 - 1644).

Mu Family Compound

Would you like to see how a wealthy landlord lived in northern China in the past? Then, a good place to visit is the Mù 牟 Family Compound, situated in Qīxiá 栖霞, Yāntái. The compound was first built during the reign of Emperor Yōngzhèng 雍正 of the Qīng 清 Dynasty (1616 - 1911), and finally completed in 1935 just prior to the Japanese invasion of China. Covering an area of 20,000 square metres with over 480 rooms the Mù Family Compound was used by the Communist Party as an example to show how landlords got rich. Like many other landlords, Mù Mòlín 牟墨林 bought huge pieces of land owned by farmers when there were natural disasters like famine. The Mù family paid those who were dying of hunger by giving them grain instead of money, and acquired the land cheaply.

Zhoucun

Honored by the Qīng 清 Emperor Qián Lóng 乾隆 as "the Number One Village in China," Zhōucūn 周村 best

Penglai Pavillion is situated on majestic cliffs facing the sea.

A granary in the Mu Family Compound

The Mu Family, like many wealthy Chinese families from the old times, had a stage for Peking Opera performances on its huge estate.

exemplifies how small cities in China have been able to accumulate wealth over the years. Zhōucūn has a history of over 6,000 years and was in the heartland of the State of Qí 齐, a state in the Zhōu 周 Dynasty (1046 - 256 B.C.E.). Once part of Zībó 淄博, which is historically known as "the Porcelain and Ceramics Capital of the North China" and also a center for the textile industry, Zhōucūn gradually developed itself into a distribution center in northern China. During its most affluent and successful period between the Míng (1368 - 1644) 明 and Qīng (1616 - 1911) dynasties, Zhōucūn had over 5,000 trading companies dealing in money transfer, and the production of grain, silk, cotton and daily household supplies. Businessmen from all over the country came to set up franchises here, including bankers from Shānxī 山西 Province and Huīzhōu 徽州 merchants from southern Ānhuī 安徽 Province. Rich families of Zhōucūn had their shops and goods distributed in all major cities. For example, the Mèng 孟 family opened a high-end silk shop called Ruìfúxiáng 瑞蚨祥 in Běijīng 北京. Architecture from the Míng and Qīng dynasties has been well preserved. Zhōucūn has become a popular destination for Visitors be-

Architecture from the Ming and Qing dynasties has been well-preserved in Zhoucun.

55

cause it provides a glimpse into an early form of capitalism in north China.

Qi Great Wall

Prior to the first Chinese Emperor Qín Shǐ Huáng who started the construction of the Great Wall, there was another wall undulating Shāndōng Province, known as the Qí Great Wall. About 600 kilometers long, the wall stretches from Chángqīng 长清 County to Zhūchéng 诸城 City. It was constructed to protect the State of Qí from the State of Chǔ 楚, a very powerful state during the Spring and Autumn Period (770 - 476 B.C.E.). Nowadays, the Qí Great Wall is of high interest to tourists with an archaeological and military perspective.

Outside a curio shop in Zhoucun

The Qi Great Wall, stretching from west to east in Shandong, was built during the Spring and Autumn Period (770 - 476 B.C.E.).

The magnificent city gate of Qufu

Explore Shandong Tours

The capital, the mountain and the saint
Jǐnán 济南 — Mt. Tài (in Jǐníng 济宁) — Qūfǔ 曲阜

You see the very best of Shāndōng 山东 following this route. Start the trip in the "spring city" of Jǐnán. Take a walk around Dàmíng Hú 大明湖 (lake) while there. Then prepare yourself for the long climb up the famous Mt. Tài (Tàishān 泰山). Confucius once said that on top of Tàishān, you can feel the smallness of the world. Not far from the mountains is the city of Qūfǔ, the birthplace of Confucius. The mansion, the temple and the cemetery of Confucius are all worth a visit. While in Qūfǔ, taste some delicately prepared Confucian dishes like Supreme Bean Curd.

Suggested Timeline: 5 days

Coastal cities
Qīngdǎo 青岛 — Wēihǎi 威海 — Yāntái 烟台 — Qīxiá 栖霞 — Pénglái 蓬莱

Traveling along the coast of Shāndōng is fun, especially for the leisurely tourist. Begin the trip with a day at the beaches of Qīngdǎo or a climb of Láoshān 崂山 (Láo Mountain). Sea animal lovers shouldn't miss Qīngdǎo Polar Ocean World, probably the best aquarium in China. Then drive to the very east end of China, the city of Róngchéng 荣成 (part of Wēihǎi). Between Wēihǎi and Yāntái are endless vineyards that yield the country's best grapes. It's said that the fragrance of the grapes lingers in the air. Stay at least one night in Yāntái enjoying its breeze, seafood, and wines. If time permits, visit the Mù 牟 Family Compound in Qīxiá 栖霞 to get a glimpse of how Chinese landlords used to live. The family built over 480 rooms to house its members! From Qīxiá, go to Pénglái, known as the "Fairyland on Earth."

Suggested Timeline: 4 days

Into the culture and folk arts
Jǐnán 济南 — Zhōucūn 周村 — Zībó 淄博 — Qīngzhōu 青州 — Shòuguāng 寿光 — Wéifāng 潍坊

From Jǐnán travel to Zhōucūn. Though it was historically called a village, Zhōucūn is actually a city, known for its Míng 明 and Qīng 清 architectural buildings once used as shops. Zībó, the ancient capital of the State of Qí 齐 during the Spring and Autumn and the Warring States periods, used to be a center for making ceramics. Because it is a city full of cultural relics and remains, Zībó is worth exploring. Qīngzhōu has some of China's best Buddhist sculptures made during the Southern and Northern Dynasties (420 - 589 C.E.). If you have the time, spend a morning or afternoon at Shòuguāng to get an idea of what the new Chinese countryside looks like. Taste some fruits and vegetables that are grown using the most advanced agricultural techniques. End your tour in Wéifāng, a hub for folk arts. Talk with local folk artists and learn from them how to make kites, new year wood block paintings, paper cuts and clay toys.

Suggested Timeline: 3 to 4 days

Travel tips

1. Avoid traveling to Shāndōng during the May Day and National Day (October 1st) holidays. These two holidays are sometimes called the two "Golden Weeks" of the year, so most Chinese have a week-long holiday.

2. Shāndōng produces the country's best peanuts, which are a common ingredient in Shāndōng food. Those allergic to peanuts should ask about the ingredients in every dish, including the cooking oil.

Explore-A-Province in China®

Local Flavors

Shāndōng 山东 cuisine, also known as Lǔ Cài 鲁菜, is a leading representative of the culinary arts in northern China. It has greatly influenced the foods of Běijīng 北京, Tiānjīn 天津 and other northern provinces such as Héběi 河北, Liáoníng 辽宁, Jílín 吉林 and Hēilóngjiāng 黑龙江. With a history of almost 3,000 years, Shāndōng cuisine developed over time and flourished during the Qīng 清 Dynasty (1644 - 1911). Most of the popular restaurants in Běijīng in the late 19th century were run by people from Shāndōng, especially from Fúshān 福山, a district in Yāntái 烟台. Shāndōng chefs were among the most experienced and sought-after professionals not only in China, but also in most cosmopolitan cities throughout the world.

Shāndōng cuisine has three subcategories: the Jǐnán 济南 cuisine, the Jiāodōng 胶东 (eastern Shāndōng) cuisine and the Confucian dishes. Generally speaking, Shāndōng stands out for its wide variety of ingredients and a vast repertoire of cooking methods. The province abounds in fresh vegetables and seafood. Shāndōng cuisine has developed over 30 cooking styles including bào 爆 (quick frying), liū 熘 (quick frying with cornstarch), and pá 扒 (stewing).

Shāndōng cuisine pays particular attention to taste, texture and freshness. Most of the dishes tend to be slightly salty, crisp and bursting with flavor. People in Shāndōng love to season their dishes with onion and garlic; they also enjoy eating both raw. It is generally believed that the demeanor of Shāndōng people, pungent and direct, is reflected in the flavor of what they eat.

Shandong pancakes are loved throughout the province. They are made with the flour of sweet potato, corn, and soy beans and are as thin as paper. They are usually rolled up and eaten with green onion, cucumbers, and sometimes green peppers. It is said in Shandong that countryside women are judged by their mastery of making these pancakes.

Prawns in Brown Sauce

Prawns in Brown Sauce or hóngshāo dàxiā 红烧大虾 is a signature dish of the Jiāodōng cuisine and is one of the most popular dishes in Shāndōng because of its superb taste and bright coral color. Shāndōng is a large producer of the prawns that swim between the Bóhǎi 渤海 Sea and the Yellow Sea every spring and autumn.

Sweet and Sour Carp

Sweet and Sour Carp or tángcù lǐyú 糖醋鲤鱼 is a popular dish at banquets. Carp are first sauteed in oil and sprinkled with sweet-sour vinegar. The dish, crisp outside and tender inside, tastes fresh. People love ordering this dish because of its auspicious connotations. The character for carp, lǐ 鲤, is pronounced the same as the character lì 利, which means profit.

Supreme Bean Curd

This dish, called yīpǐn dòufu 一品豆腐, is meticulously prepared. The soup is creamy and milk-white, and the taste is fresh and tender. It is typical of the Confucian dishes that emphasize style and delicacy, and has been a favorite among the educated elites.

hóngshāo dàxiā 红烧大虾

tángcù lǐyú 糖醋鲤鱼

yīpǐn dòufu 一品豆腐

Shandong

Four Happiness Meat Balls

These meatballs are a must-try dish for big occasions. For generations, Chinese people believed that there were four kinds of happiness or sì xǐ 四喜 in their lives: timely rain after a drought (jiǔ hàn féng gān lín 久旱逢甘霖); running into a friend far away from home (tā xiāng yù gù zhī 他乡遇故知); the wedding night (dòng fáng huā zhú yè 洞房花烛夜) and success in passing the imperial examinations (jīn bǎng tí míng shí 金榜题名时). Each meat ball represents one kind of happiness, and the dish known as sì xǐ wánzi 四喜丸子 still has great appeal today.

Dezhou Braised Chicken

Nationally known for its fantastic taste thanks to the use of mushrooms, soy sauce, clove, fruit, and other ingredients, Dézhōu Braised Chicken or dézhōu pájī 德州扒鸡 is well-cooked and easily separates from the bone while the shape of the chicken is preserved.

dézhōu pájī 德州扒鸡

Deep-Fried Scorpions

Fried scorpions or zhà xiēzi 炸蝎子 are considered a famous Chinese delicacy. After being deep-fried, they taste slightly bitter and are very crunchy. Scorpions are abundant in the mountains of Yíshuǐ 沂水 County, western Shāndōng. After scorpions are collected every spring, they are boiled in salty water, then preserved in oil or sold to Chinese pharmacies to make medicine. Scorpions are believed to be very effective in preventing skin ulcers or scabies from developing.

sì xǐ wánzi 四喜丸子

zhá xiēzi 炸蝎子

Longevity Noodles and Peaches

In China, it is a custom to celebrate birthdays with longevity noodles and longevity peaches (especially for people over age 60). Few Chinese people, however, know that this tradition has a lot to do with Shāndōng 山东 Province.

Longevity Noodles

The tradition of having noodles or miàntiáo 面条 on one's birthday dates back to the Hàn 汉 Dynasty (206 B.C.E. - 220 C.E.). Once, the chef of the Hàn imperial court cooked noodles for the celebration of Emperor Wǔ Dì's 武帝 birthday. Wǔ Dì was furious when he saw that his birthday dish was so simple. Dōngfāng Shuò 东方朔, one of the emperor's trusted officials who was from Shāndōng, managed to calm him down. Dōngfāng Shuò explained that Péng Zǔ 彭祖, the legendary figure who lived to the ripe old age of 800, had a long face or "miàn cháng 面长," and that the noodles the royal chef made for Emperor Wǔ Dì were much longer than the face of Péng Zǔ. He added that the long noodles expressed a very special wish that the Emperor could live longer than Péng Zǔ. Dōngfāng Shuò's explanation pleased Emperor Wǔ Dì, who was happily thinking he could live even longer than Péng Zǔ. He joyously accepted the humble meal of his chef; he also accepted the wise advice of Dōngfāng Shuò, and enjoyed the simple birthday noodles. Thus, eating noodles to celebrate birthdays is practiced nationwide today.

chángshòu miàn 长寿面

shòutáo 寿桃

Longevity Peaches

Peaches have long been considered a godly fruit by the Chinese. The god of longevity or shòuxīng 寿星 carries this fruit in his hand. According to the *Agriculture God's Canon of Materia Medica* compiled in the Hàn Dynasty, those who eat peaches frequently will enjoy a longer life than those who don't. As good health and longevity are treasured by Chinese people particularly as they get older, they favor peaches above many other fruits.

According to legends, a Shāndōng native named Sūn Bìn 孙膑 (circa 380 - 320 B.C.E.) studied military theories with a master by the name of Guǐgǔzǐ 鬼谷子 for 12 years, and then suddenly remembered that his mother's 80th birthday was approaching. Before he left to visit his mother, Guǐgǔzǐ handed him a peach and said, "Take this peach to your mother as a birthday gift." Then an auspicious miracle happened. After Sūn Bìn's mother ate the peach, she looked much younger. All the neighbors followed Sūn Bìn's example and offered their parents peaches. When peaches are not in season, people offer big, peach-shaped buns called shòutáo 寿桃 as birthday gifts to the elderly.

59

Collector's Corner – Kites

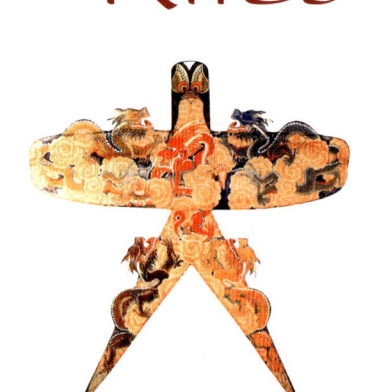

Wéifāng 潍坊, a city in eastern Shāndōng Province, is known as the Kite Capital of the World. It was here that the first forms of kites appeared 2,300 years ago. It is said that Mò Zǐ 墨子 (468 - 376 B.C.E.), founder of Mohism and a Wéifāng native, made a wooden eagle that took him three years to complete, and flew it for only one day. Then, his friend Lǔ Bān 鲁班, a great inventor of the time, successfully flew a magpie made of bamboo for three days. Kites at that time were used mainly for military purposes and were called yuān 鸢 in northern China and yào 鹞 in southern China.

Kites became accessible to the general public beginning in the Táng 唐 Dynasty (618 - 907 C.E.). Then, they were brought to Japan by monks, and later to southeastern Asian countries. Marco Polo, the adventurer who traveled to the East introduced kites to Europe. The Míng 明 and Qīng 清 dynasties saw the peak of Chinese kites. Cities like Wéifāng, Běijīng 北京, Tiānjīn 天津, and Nántōng 南通 grew into important centers for designing, making, and trading kites around the world.

Kite flying involves many traditions. Usually people start flying kites in early April to welcome the coming of the spring. As one saying goes, "On the third of March (the third month in the lunar calendar), many kites in the sky (yòu shì yī nián sān yuè sān, fēng zhēng fēi mǎn tiān 又是一年三月三，风筝飞满天)." This kite flying day is around the fifth or sixth of April, also a holiday in China called Qīngmíng 清明 (the sweeping of the graves day). In cities like Běijīng and Tiānjīn, people fly kites hoping to get rid of bad luck. As kite flying is closely associated with Qīngmíng, a festival during which Chinese people worship ancestors, it was banned because it was not seen as revolutionary or communist during the Cultural Revolution (1966 - 1976).

An old woodblock print from Yangliuqing, Tianjin. The ten women who are flying kites are supposed to be the most beautiful ladies in Chinese history.

The city of Weifang is the world's "Capital of Kites." It is believed that the first kite in history was made here.

Farmers are hired to work in the numerous kite workshops in Weifang.

Shandong

Beautiful kites from Weifang

Step-by-step Kite Making

Making kites is fun! Follow these instructions:

1. Prepare the overall kite design.
2. Cut the bamboo and assemble the frame according to the design.
3. Secure the frame by gluing and reinforcing it with string.
4. Prepare the design on the paper or silk.
5. Paint the design by hand.
6. Cut out the parts of the kite.
7. Glue the paper/silk parts onto the bamboo frame.
8. Trim and secure the kite.
9. Prepare the string, reel, and tail and attach them to the kite.

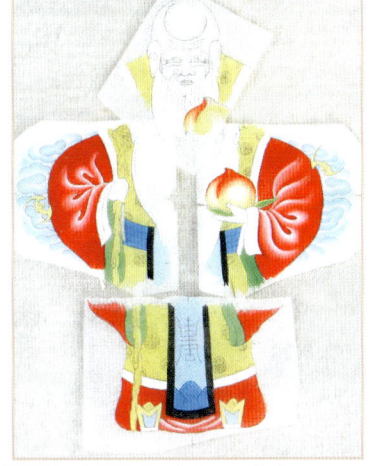

(Text and images taken from *Chinese Traditional Holidays and Festivals* by OCDF Publications showing Mr. Kǒng Bǐngzhāng 孔炳彰, a top kite-maker in Běijīng 北京.)

Weifang Kite Museum

The largest kite museum in the world, Wéifāng 潍坊 Kite Museum covers 8,100 sq m. The design of the entire building looks like the dragon head of a centipede kite, one of the most famous kite styles of Wéifāng. The museum displays over 1,000 valuable kites from history.

References

Books:

中国地图册(中英文版)，成都地图出版社，2007年
中国人民共和国行政区划简册，中国地图出版社，2007年
现代汉语词典(第五版)，商务印书馆，2006年
中国百家姓寻根游，黄利，陕西师范大学出版社，2004年
中国城市人性格地图，郭俊，万卷出版公司，2006年
问吧，杨庆茹 吴智勇等，中华书局，2007年
走遍中国：山东，走遍中国编辑部，中国旅游出版社，2007年
趣闻山东，王晨光主编，旅游教育出版社，2007年
山东知行书，张志刚，广东旅游出版社，2007年
中国导游十万个为什么：山东，曾招喜，张爱文，中国旅游出版社，2007年
解读山东人，刘德增，中国文联出版社，2006年
中国民俗大系：山东民俗，叶涛，甘肃人民出版社，2004年
山东居住民俗，山曼主编，济南出版社，2006年
齐鲁民间造型艺术，孔新苗，山东画报出版社，2005年

Yin Zhongqing. 2007. *The Political System of China*. China International Press

Dang Guoying. 2006. *Agricultural, Rural Areas and Farmers in China*. China International Press

Jason Patent. 2007. *Philosophies & Religions in China*. OCDF Publications

Jason Patent. 2007. *Chinese Myths and Legends*. OCDF Publications

Zhi E'xiang. 2005. *The Basics of Traditional Chinese Culture*. Foreign Languages Press

Lee Siow Mong. 1995. *Sprectrum of Chinese Culture*. Pelanduk Publications

Xu Yuanxiang. 2007. Confucius: *A Philosopher for the Ages*. China Intercontinental Press

Websites:

About.com, *http://chineseculture.about.com*
China Internet Information Center, *http://www.china.org.cn/english*
China Knowledge, *www.chinaknowledge.edu*
中国网, *www.china.com.cn*
China Cultural Net Information, *www.cnt.com.cn*
Shandong Provincial Government, *www.shandong.gov.cn*
Shandong Tourism Bureau, *www. travelshandong.us*

Topical References

Provincial History
Wei Tang. 1984. *Legends and Tales from History*. China Reconstructs
M.E.H. "Jiang Taigong: The Supreme Strategist," *http://www.jadedragon.com/archives*
CRI English, "Why Did Xu Fu Go to Japan?" *http://english.cri.cn*
Ad Blankestijn, "Japan as the Promised Land: Xu Fu and Shingu," *http://www.interculturaljapan.com*
Cycnet.com, "Fang Xuanling," *www.cycnet.com/encyclopedia/history*
Spartacus Schoolnet, "Jiang Qing," *http://www.spartaxus.schoolnet.co.uk/CHINAjiang.htm*

Provincial Socioeconomy
Hsien-Shen Wen. 2007. "Shandong Province: The Next Big Thing." *www.cw.tom.tw/english*

中国网. "Agricultural in Shandong Marches into Global Market," *http://www.china.org.cn/english/2002/Feb/26383.htm*
Shouguang Government, *www.shouguang.gov.cn*

Provincial Capital
Jinan Government, *www.jinan.gov.cn*
Yantai Government, *www.yantai.gov.cn*
Weihai Government, *www.weihai.gov.cn*
Jining Government, *www.jining.gov.cn*
Weifang Government, *www.weifang.gov.cn*
Zibo Government, *www.zibo.gov.cn*
Dezhou Government, *www.dezhou.gov.cn*
Heze Government, *www.heze.gov.cn*

Provincial Heritage
Gong Dafei and Feng Yu. 1994. *Chinese Maxims*. Sinolingua
Yao Dan. 2006. Chinese Literature. China International Press
Deng Yinke. 2005. *Ancient Chinese Inventions*. China International Press
Liao Yuquan. 2006. *Traditional Chinese Medicine*. China International Press
Xinhua source, "Ancient China also cared about female sexual pleasure," *http://English.peopledaily.com.cn*
Bradley Winterton, "Looking at Jin Ping Mei in light of Taiwan's sexual revolution," *www.taipeitimes.com*

Special Feature
Qu Chunli. 1996. *The Life of Confucius*. Foreign Languages Press
Xu Yuanxiang. 2007. *Confucius: A Philosopher for the Ages*. China International Press
Xu Yuanxiang and Zhang Bing. 2007. *Mencius: A Benevolent Saint for the Ages*. China International Press
Yao Dan. 2006. *Chinese Literature*. China International Press
J. D. Brown. 2000. *China: the 50 Most Memorable Trips*. Frommer's

Provincial Highlights
New World Press. 1980. *60 Scenic Wonders in China*. New World Press
"Cultural of China" Editorial Board. 2002. *Famous Mountains and Rivers*. Foreign Languages Press
The Taoist Association of China. 2002. *Taoism*. Foreign Languages Press
Jin Zhilin. 2004. *Chinese Folk Arts*. China International Press
Liu Zhongmin. 2002. *Folk Handicrafts*. Foreign Languages Press
Yang Xianrang and Yang Yang. 2000. *Chinese Folk Art*. New World Press
Huang Jian and Guo Qiuhui. 2006. *Chinese Arts & Crafts*. China International Press
Dongying Government, *www.dongying.gov.cn*
Shandong Tourism Bureau, *www. travelshandong.us*
Zhucheng Government, *www.zhucheng.gov.cn*
China Internet Information Center, "Shandong Cuisine," *http://china.org.cn/english/imperial/26127.htm*
Chinadaily.com.cn, "Shandong Cuisine," *www.chinadaily.com.cn*

The above websites listed as references were checked November 2007 - July 2008.

Shandong

Acknowledgements

Special thanks to Mr. Zhai Jian for contributing seven key photographs to this book.

Special thanks to Mr. Liu Gang for contributing the story and images of the paper cut couple to this book.

Special thanks to Mr. Huadexiang for his participation to this book.

Special thanks to Mr. Qin Junxiao, president of China Tushu Publishing Ltd., for his participation to this book.

Unless otherwise noted, all translations were done by Paris Lambrou, Sui Hong and Megan Zaroda.

Unless otherwise noted in Picture Credits, all photos © Chinese Photo Gallery and © Phototime

Unless otherwise noted, all images © OCDF Publications Archives

Picture Credits

Chen Weifeng 陈为峰, Chen Yunpei 陈允沛, Da Ri 大日, Dong Naide 董乃德, Fan Yongqiu 范咏秋, He Lijun 何立军, He Peiyu 贺培玉, Hua Dexiang 华德祥, Huang Jianqing 黄建清, Hui Hui 辉辉, Jiang Fuxiang 姜福祥, Jiang Hanfeng 江汉风, Li Qiang 李强, Li Wei 李伟, Li Zhuo 李茁, Lin Shu 林舒, Liu Gang 刘刚, Ming Xueying 明雪影, Mu Jun 穆军, Qi Yan 戚岩, Qiuyu 秋雨, Seyingpeng 色影鹏, Sun Jiayong 孙家勇, Sun Qi 孙琦, Wei Dong 魏东, Xing Changrui 邢昌瑞, Xuelanghu 雪狼湖, Wang Zhige 王之阁, Yan Minglei 严明磊, Yang lili 杨力利, Yao Qunsheng 姚群生, Yin Ming 殷明, Zhou Jiafu 周家富, Zhai Jian 翟健, Zhang Xisheng 张佃生, Zhang Jianjun 张建军, Zhang Qingmin 张庆民, Zhao Qiuming 赵秋明, Zhi Yuntian 志云田, Zhuang Zi 庄子

Jane Liedtke, welcom 321, Qilu Wanxiang 齐鲁万象, Yiwang Chuanmei 亿网传媒, Youshi Huanghun 又是黄昏, Zhangjianfeng 掌见风

Weifang Kite Factory
www.wf-kite.com
潍坊风筝厂

Countryside fair

Sacrificing to the Dragon King

Every March 18 on the Chinese lunar calendar or April 10 on the Gregorian calendar, fishermen in Zhōugēzhuāng 周戈庄 Village, Qīngdǎo 青岛, gather in front of the Temple of the Dragon King to offer sacrifices and pray for a safe and prosperous year. This day, called gǔyǔ 谷雨, marks the first day of the men's sea journeys for the year. For sacrifices, they offer pigs decorated in red, and their wives prepare big buns with vividly-made shrimp, prawn, fish and crab.

With all the fishing boats neatly lined up nearby, captains and their crews kneel down to face the sea and kowtow. This whole process delivers a message to the Dragon King, who is believed to be living in the deep sea. The men are going to take what belongs to the Dragon King from the sea, but they are asking for his understanding and for his permission and for his blessing.

The tradition of sacrificing to the sea or jìhǎi 祭海 in the Qīngdǎo area dates back 500 years. It is often coupled with yānggē 秧歌 dance, land-boat (hànchuán 旱船) and waist drum (yāogǔ 腰鼓) dances.

Fireworks are lit to mark the voyage.

Pigs and roosters are decorated and offered as sacrifices to the Dragon King.

Yangge dancer

People burn incense while they pray.

Fishermen's wives prepare big buns with beautiful decoration.